# Sing-Along Favorites for
# ACCORDION

ARRANGED BY GARY MEISNER

D0613497

ISBN 978-1-4584-0697-2

## HAL•LEONARD®
## CORPORATION

7777 W. BLUEMOUND RD. P.O. BOX 13819 MILWAUKEE, WI 53213

In Australia Contact:
**Hal Leonard Australia Pty. Ltd.**
4 Lentara Court
Cheltenham, Victoria, 3192 Australia
Email: ausadmin@halleonard.com.au

Visit Hal Leonard Online at
**www.halleonard.com**

# CONTENTS

# AMERICA, THE BEAUTIFUL

Words by KATHERINE LEE BATES
Music by SAMUEL A. WARD

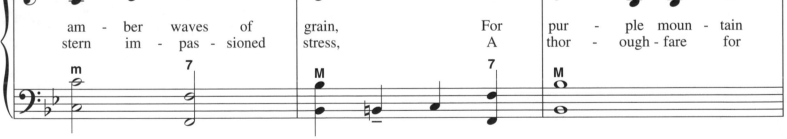

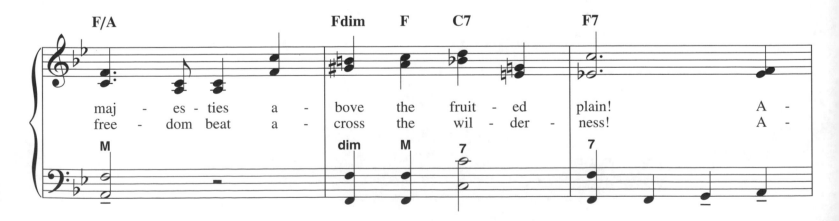

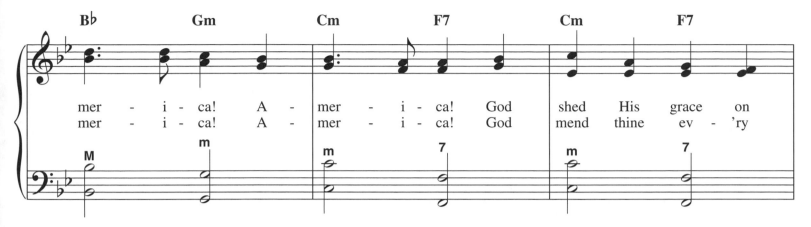

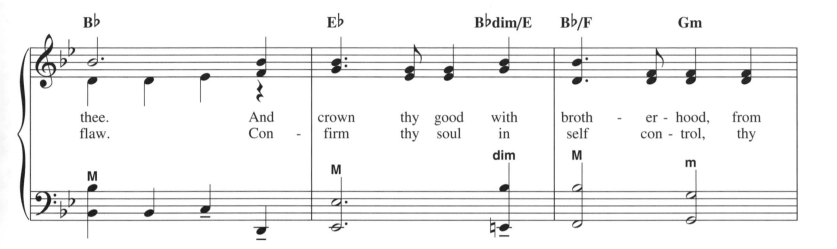

*Additional Lyrics*

3. O beautiful for heroes proved
   In liberating strife,
   Who more than self their country loved
   And mercy more than life!
   America! America!
   May God thy gold refine
   'Til all success be nobleness
   And every gain divine.

4. O beautiful for patriot dream
   That sees beyond the years;
   Thine alabaster cities gleam
   Undimmed by human tears.
   America! America!
   God shed His grace on thee,
   And crown thy good with brotherhood,
   From sea to shining sea.

# BEAUTIFUL BROWN EYES

Traditional

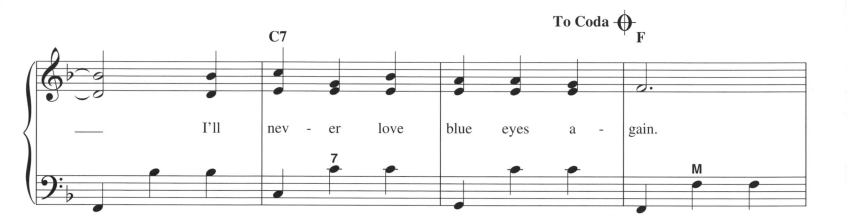

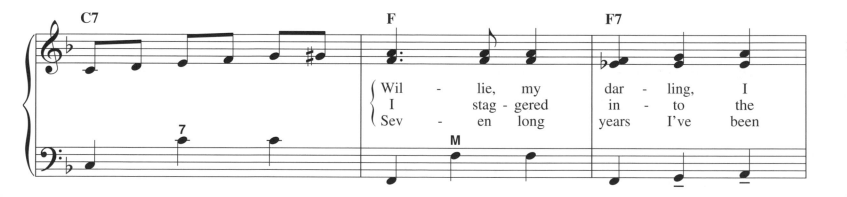

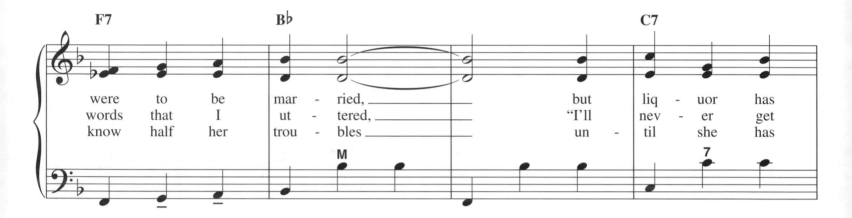

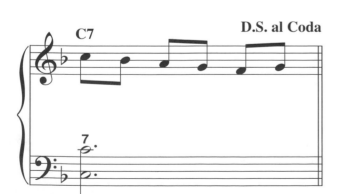

# DOWN BY THE RIVERSIDE

African American Spiritual

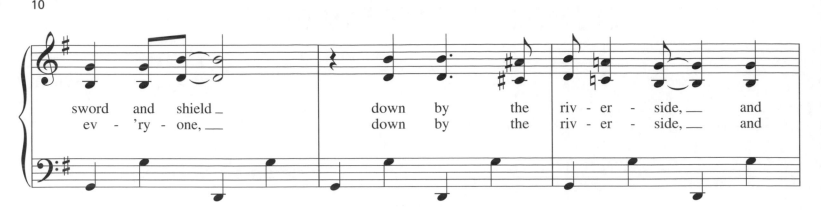

sword and shield
ev - 'ry - one, ___

down by the riv - er - side, ___ and
down by the riv - er - side, ___ and

D7          G

stud - y ___ war no more. ___ I ain't gon - na
stud - y ___ war no more. ___

7

**Chorus**
C          G

stud - y war no more, I ain't gon - na stud - y war no

M          M

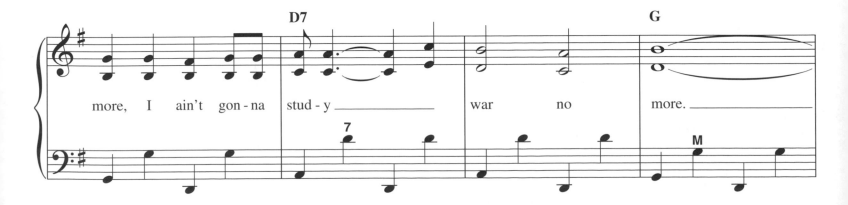

D7          G

more, I ain't gon - na stud - y ___ war no more. ___

7          M

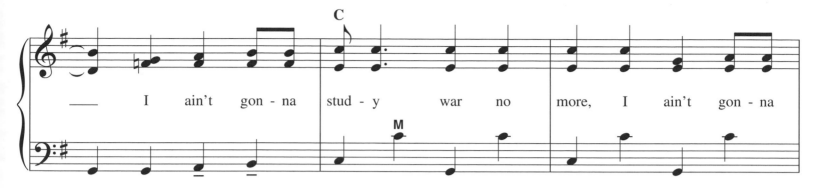

*Additional Lyrics*

3. Gonna try on my long white robe
   Down by the riverside,
   Down by the riverside,
   Down by the riverside.
   Gonna try on my long white robe
   Down by the riverside
   And study war no more.
   *Chorus*

4. Gonna walk with the Prince of Peace
   Down by the riverside,
   Down by the riverside,
   Down by the riverside.
   Gonna walk with the Prince of Peace
   Down by the riverside
   And study war no more.
   *Chorus*

# BY THE LIGHT OF THE SILVERY MOON

Lyrics by ED MADDEN
Music by GUS EDWARDS

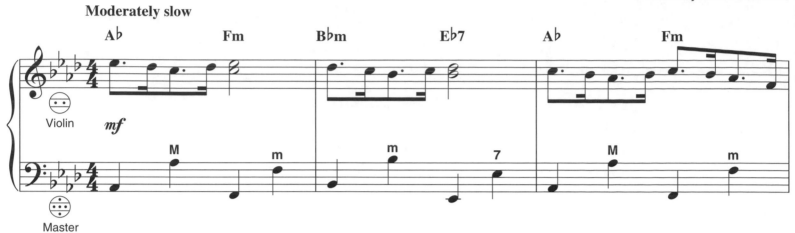

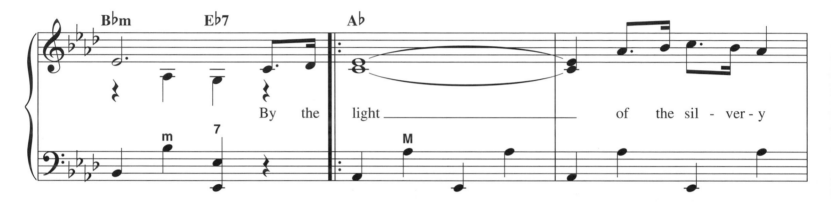

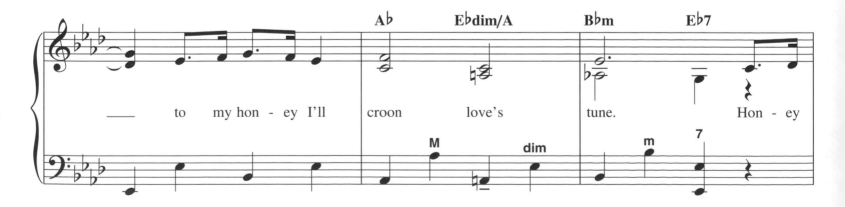

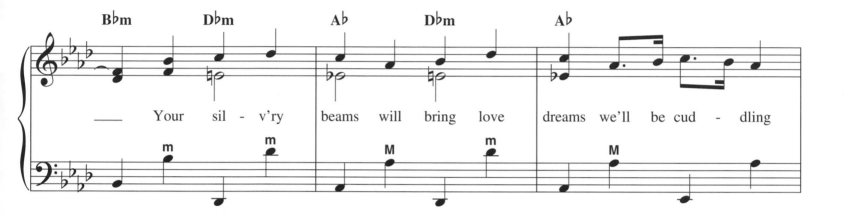

# (Oh, My Darling)
# CLEMENTINE

Words and Music by
PERCY MONTROSE

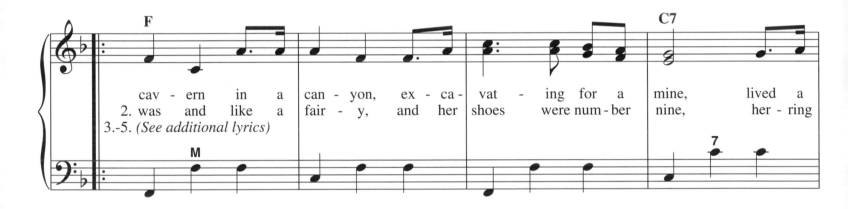

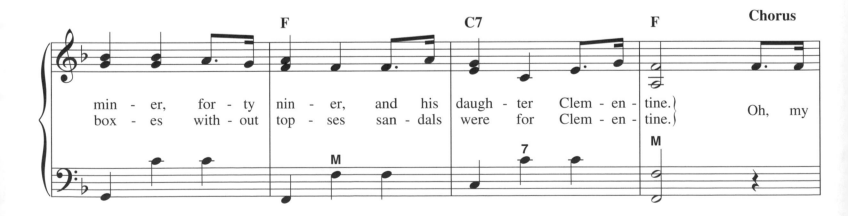

dar - ling, oh, my dar - ling, oh, my dar - ling Clem - en - tine! You are

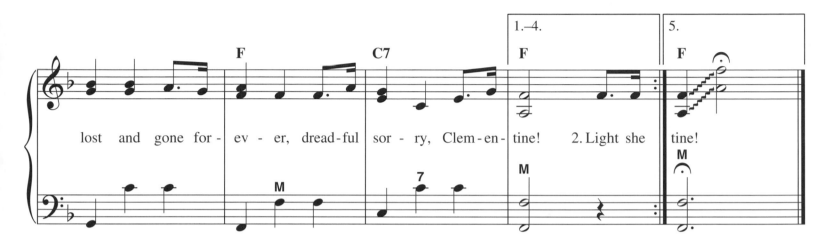

lost and gone for - ev - er, dread-ful sor - ry, Clem-en - tine! 2. Light she tine!

*Additional Lyrics*

3. Drove she ducklings to the water
   Ev'ry morning just at nine.
   Hit her foot against a splinter,
   Fell into the foaming brine.
   *Chorus*

4. Ruby lips above the water,
   Blowing bubbles soft and fine.
   Alas for me! I was no swimmer,
   So I lost my Clementine.
   *Chorus*

5. There's a churchyard on the hillside
   Where the flowers grow and twine,
   There grow roses 'mongst the posies
   Fertilized by Clementine.
   *Chorus*

# CUDDLE UP A LITTLE CLOSER, LOVEY MINE

from THE THREE TWINS

Words by OTTO HARBACH
Music by KARL HOSCHNA

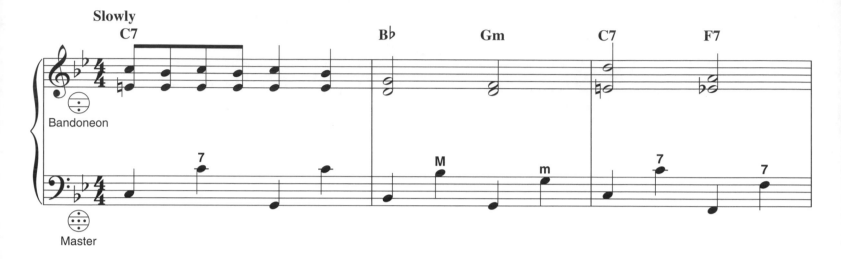

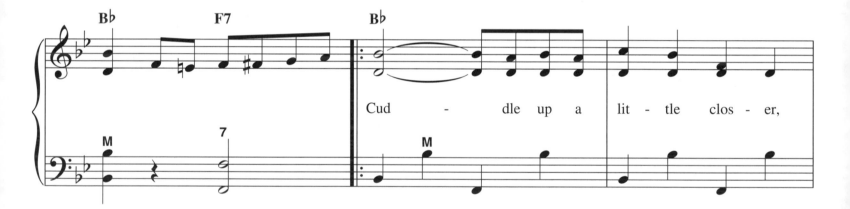

be my lit - tle cling - ing vine.

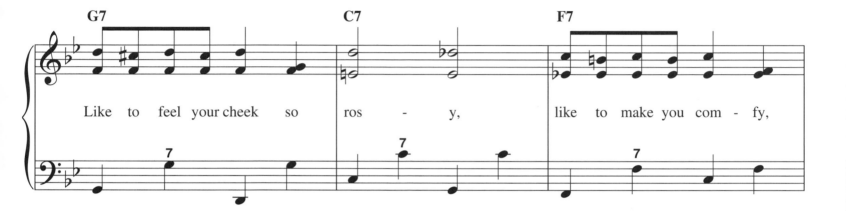

Like to feel your cheek so ros - y, like to make you com - fy,

co - zy. 'Cause I love from head to toe - sy,

lov - ey mine. mine.

# DOWN IN THE VALLEY

Traditional American Folksong

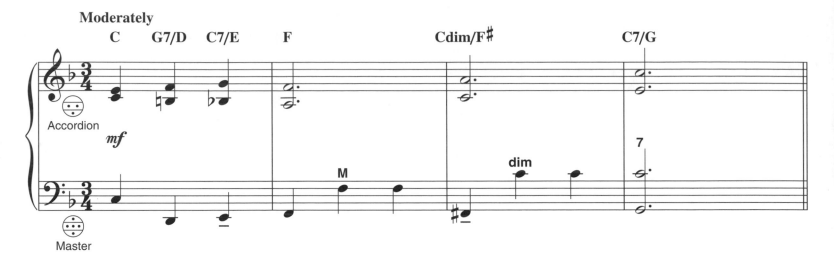

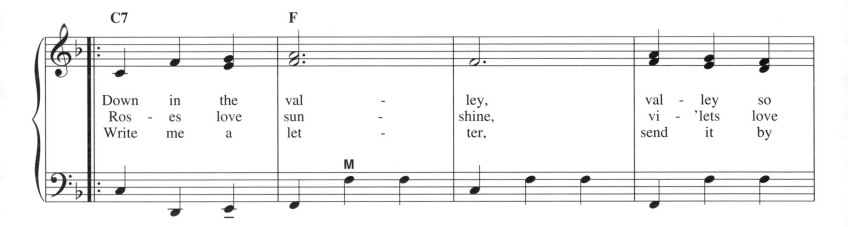

Down in the val - ley, val - ley so
Ros - es love sun - shine, vi - 'lets so
Write me a let - ter, send it by

low, _____ late in the eve -
dew, _____ an - gels in heav -
mail; _____ send it in care

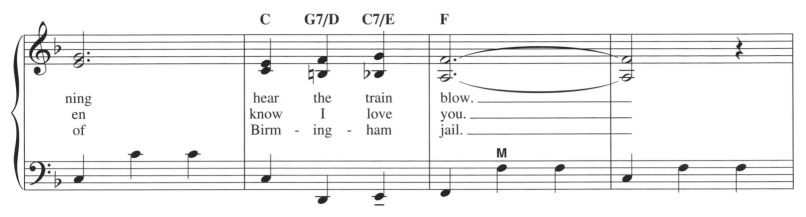

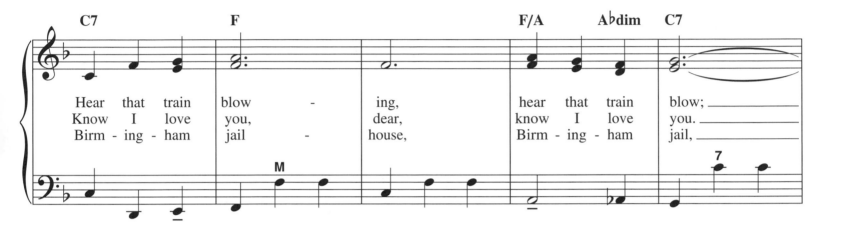

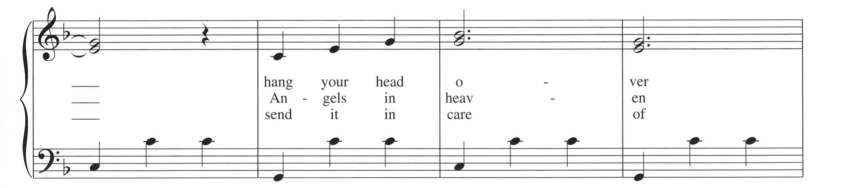

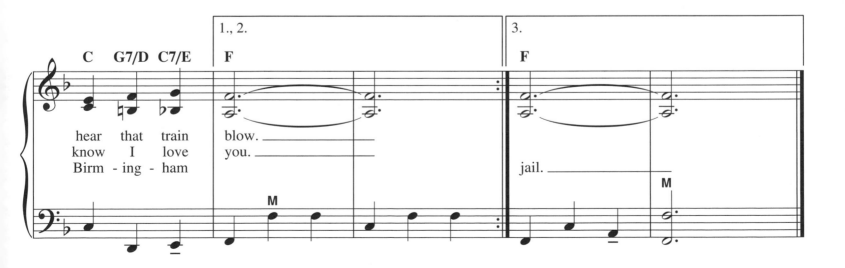

# FOR HE'S A JOLLY GOOD FELLOW

Traditional

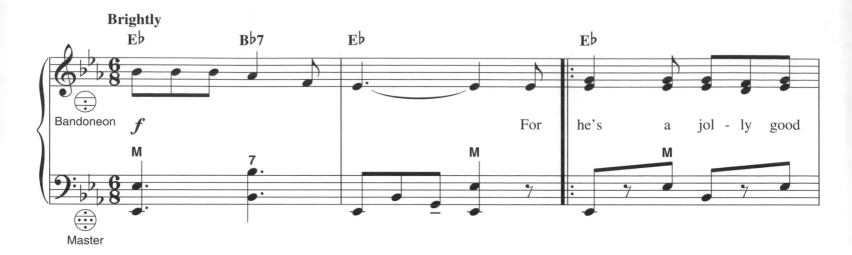

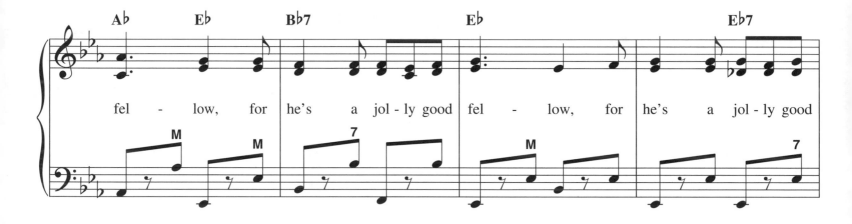

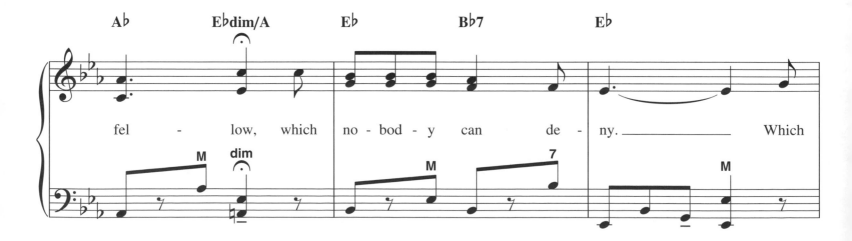

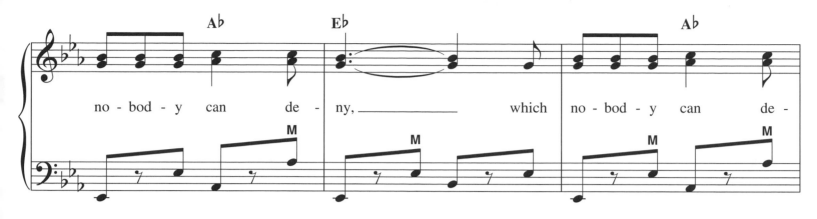

no-bod-y can de - ny, _____ which no-bod-y can de-

ny. _____ For he's a jol - ly good fel - low, for

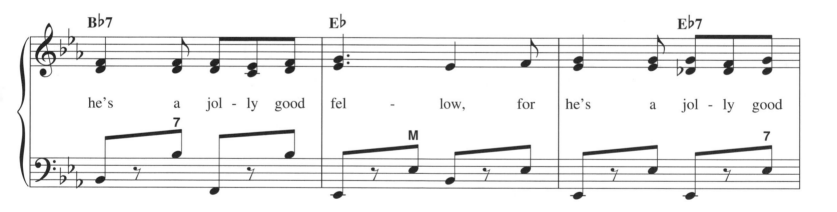

he's a jol - ly good fel - low, for he's a jol - ly good

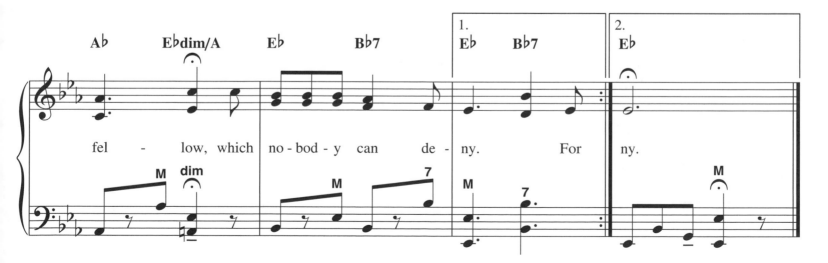

fel - low, which no-bod-y can de - ny. For ny.

# FOR ME AND MY GAL

from FOR ME AND MY GAL

Words by EDGAR LESLIE and E. RAY GOETZ
Music by GEORGE W. MEYER

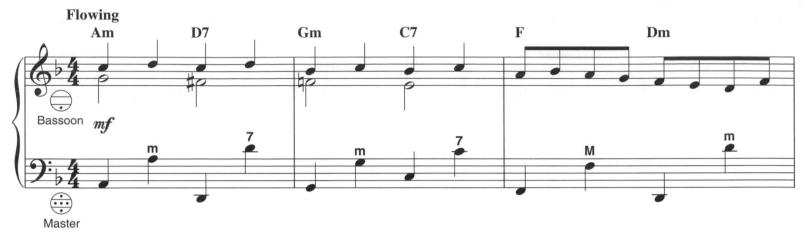

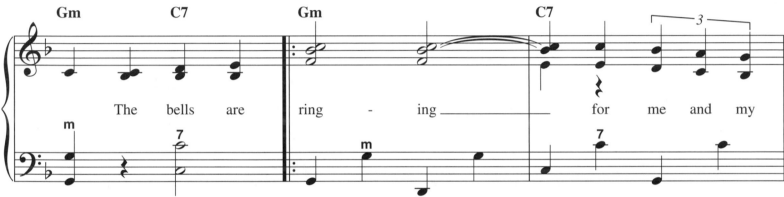

The bells are ring - ing _____ for me and my

gal. _____ The birds are sing - ing _____

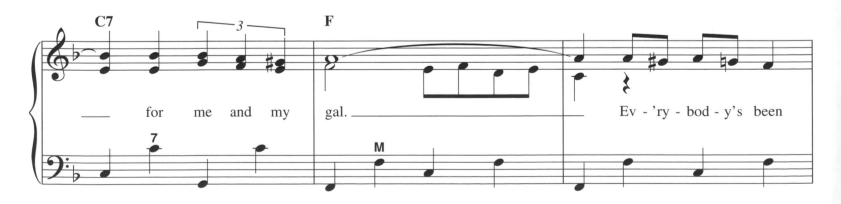

_____ for me and my gal. _____ Ev - 'ry - bod - y's been

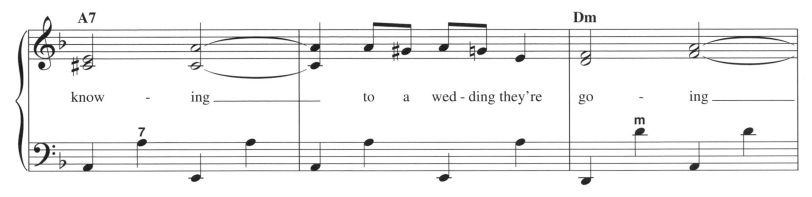

know - ing _____ to a wed - ding they're go - ing _____

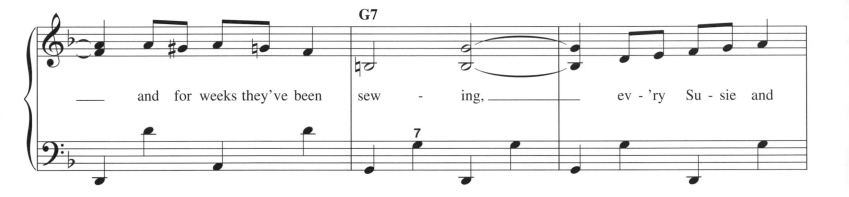

_____ and for weeks they've been sew - ing, _____ ev - 'ry Su - sie and

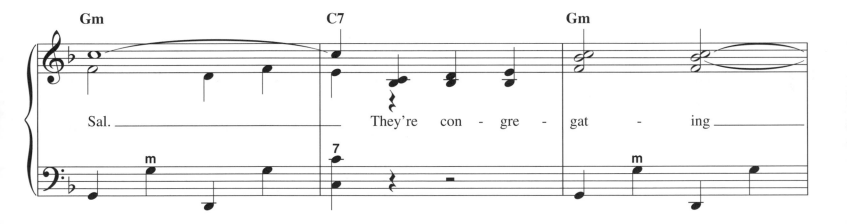

Sal. _____ They're con - gre - gat - ing _____

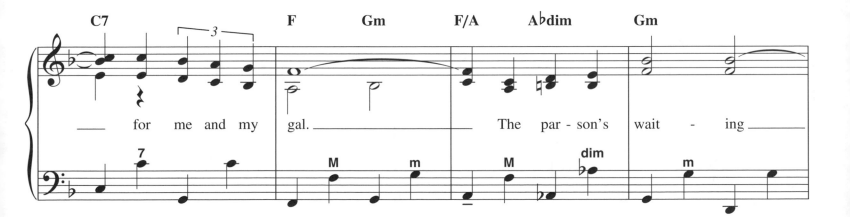

_____ for me and my gal. _____ The par - son's wait - ing _____

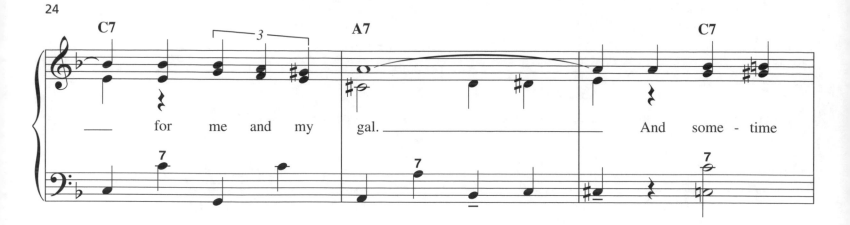

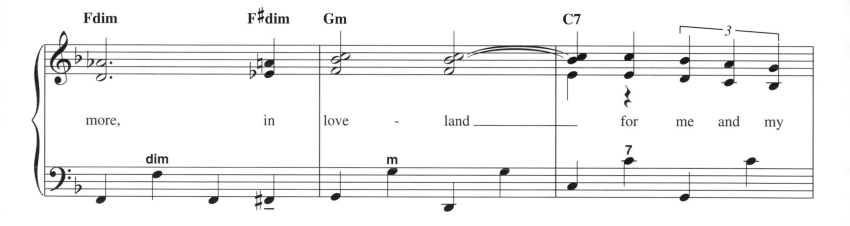

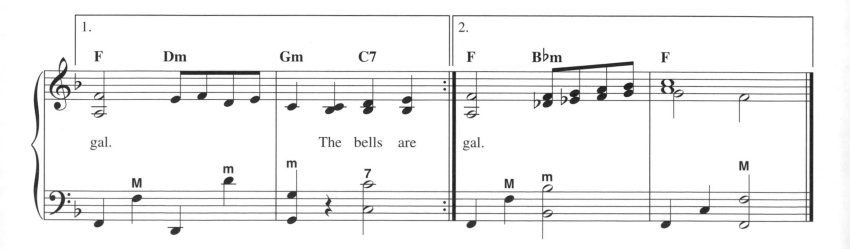

# HOME ON THE RANGE

Lyrics by DR. BREWSTER HIGLEY
Music by DAN KELLY

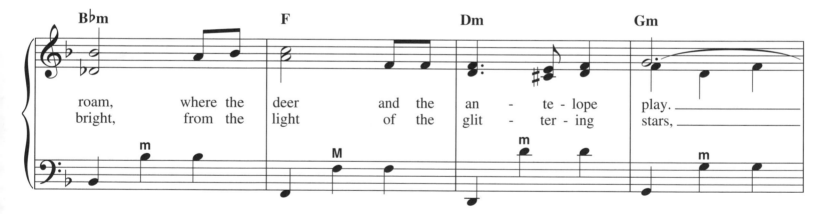

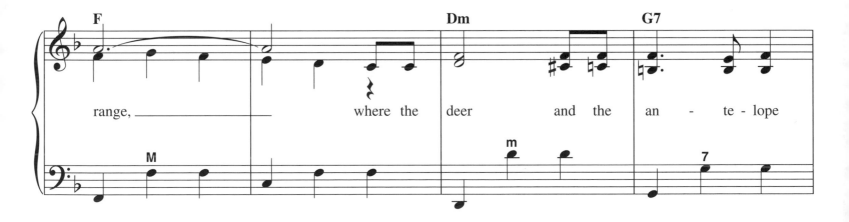

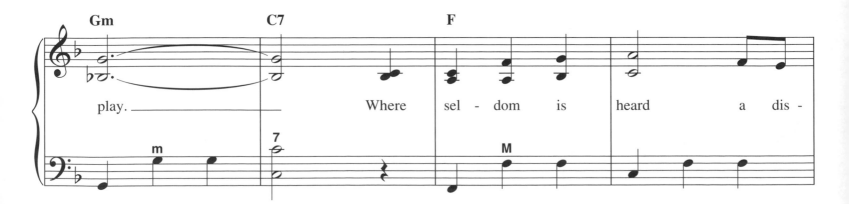

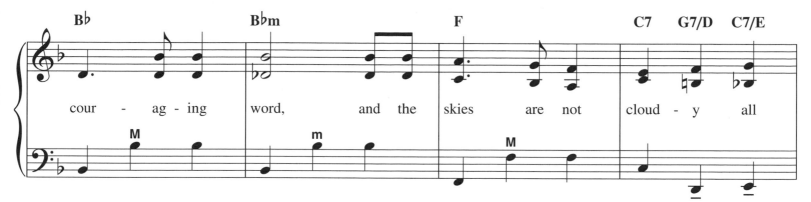

cour - ag - ing word, and the skies are not cloud - y all

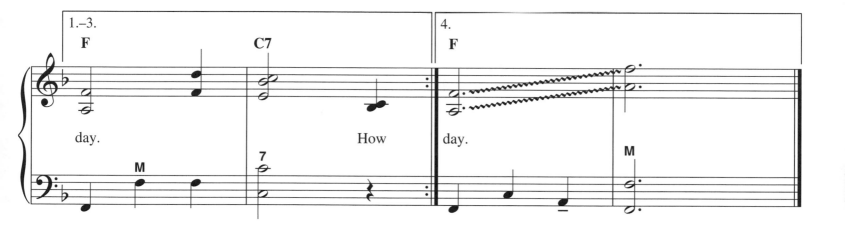

day. How day.

*Additional Lyrics*

3. Where the air is so pure and the zephyrs so free,
   And the breezes so balmy and light;
   Oh, I would not exchange my home on the range
   For the glittering cities so bright.
   *Chorus*

4. Oh, give me a land where the bright diamond sand
   Flows leisurely down with the stream,
   Where the graceful white swan glides slowly along,
   Like a maid in a heavenly dream.
   *Chorus*

# HAIL, HAIL, THE GANG'S ALL HERE

Words by D.A. ESROM
Music by THEODORE F. MORSE
and ARTHUR SULLIVAN

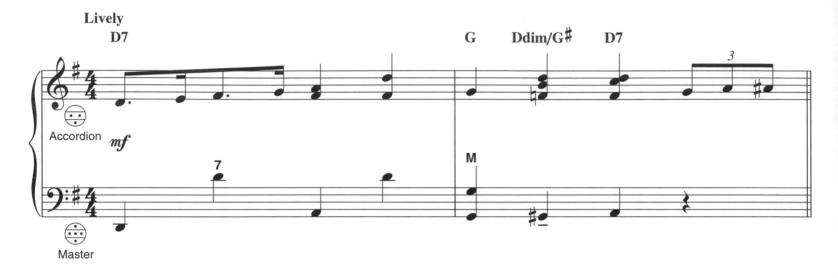

Hail! Hail! The gang's all here. What the heck do we care,

what the heck do we care? Hail! Hail! The gang's all here.

What the heck do we care now! Hail! Hail! The

gang's all here. What the heck do we care,

what the heck do we care? Hail! Hail! The gang's all here.

1.
What the heck do we care now.

2.
now.

# I LOVE YOU TRULY

Words and Music by
CARRIE JACOBS-BOND

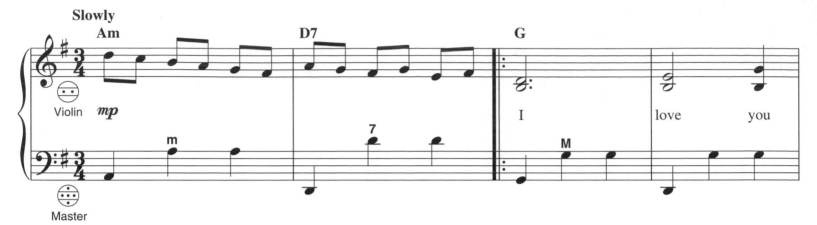

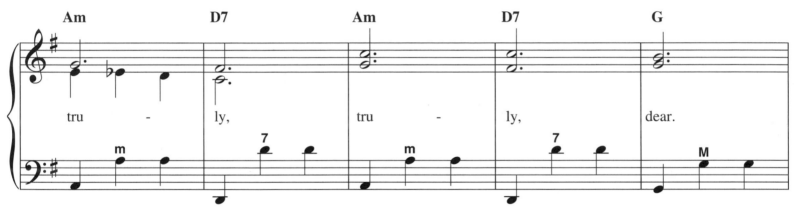

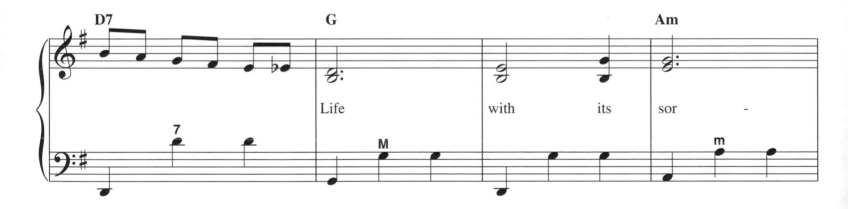

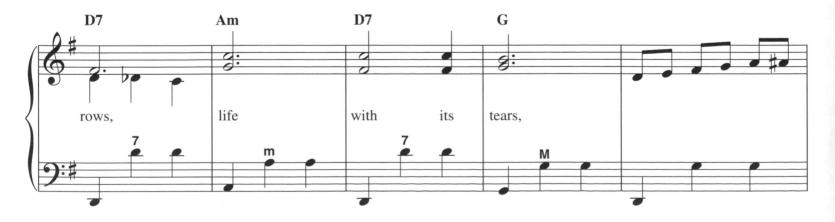

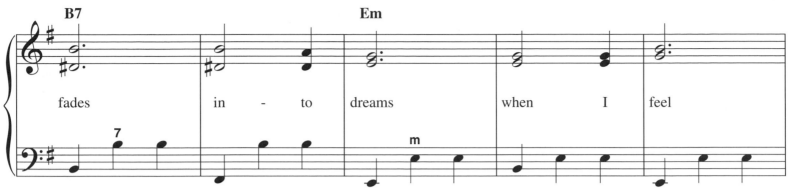

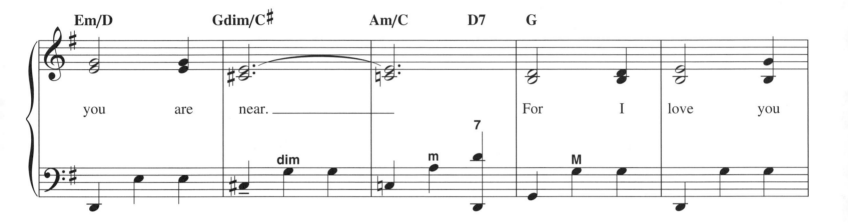

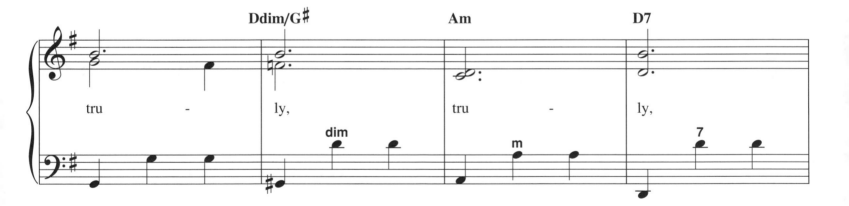

# I WANT A GIRL
### (Just Like the Girl that Married Dear Old Dad)

Words by WILLIAM DILLON
Music by HARRY VON TILZER

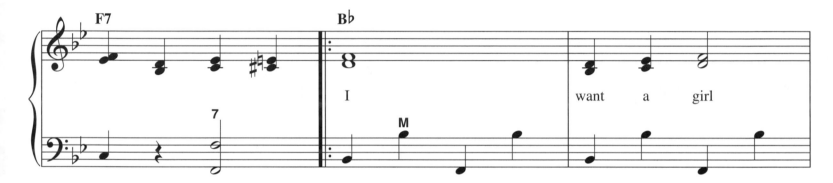

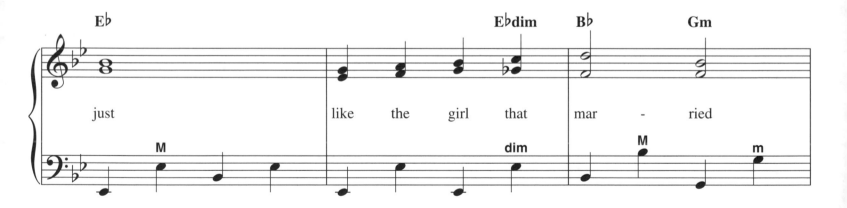

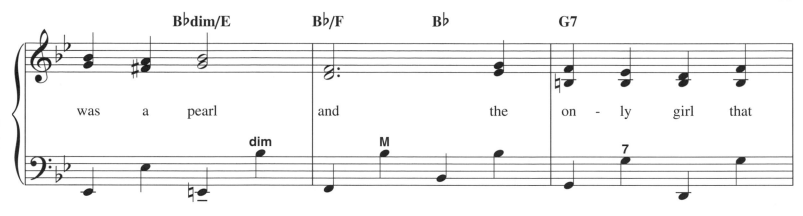

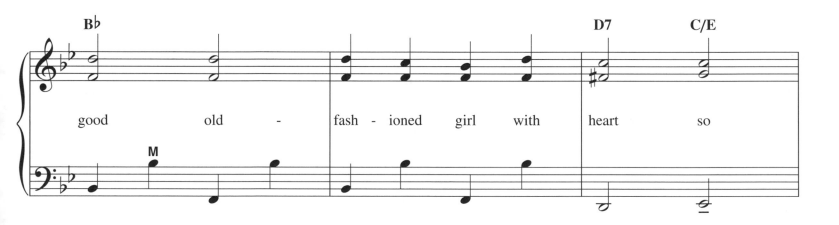

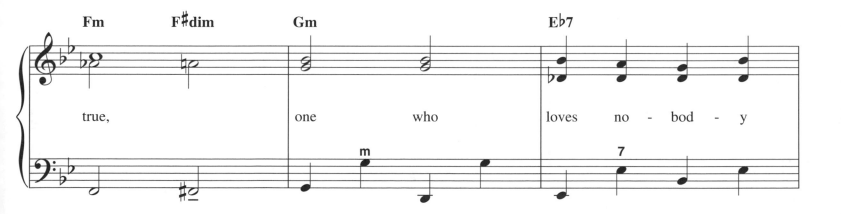

else but you. I

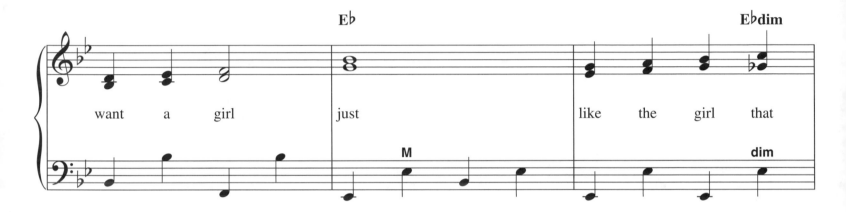

want a girl just like the girl that

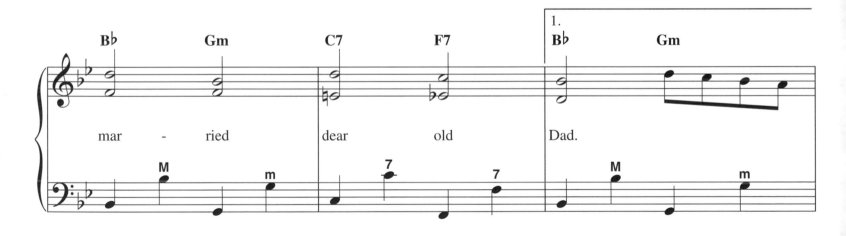

mar - ried dear old Dad.

Dad.

# MARGIE

Words by BENNY DAVIS
Music by CON CONRAD
and J. RUSSELL ROBINSON

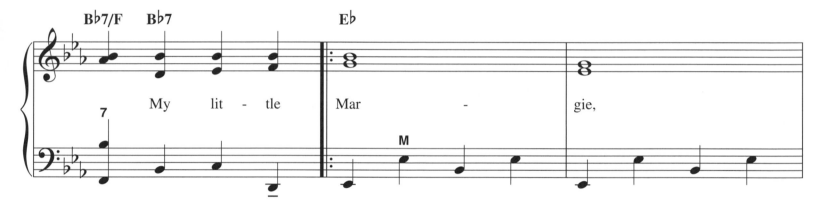

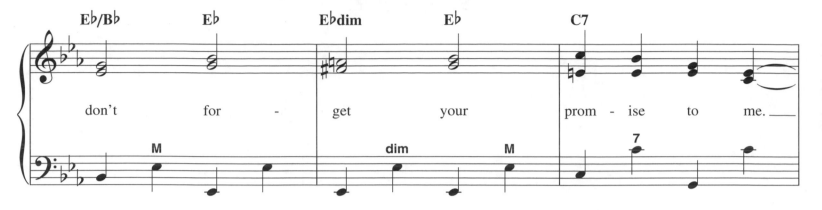

don't for - get your prom - ise to me. ___

___ I have bought a

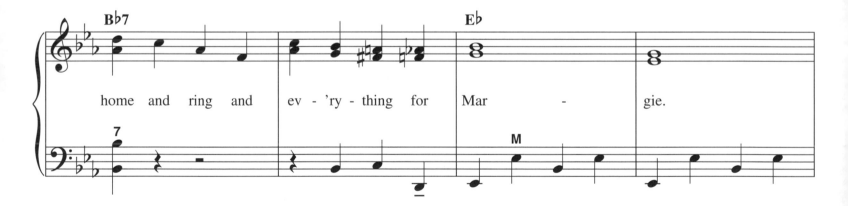

home and ring and ev - 'ry - thing for Mar - gie.

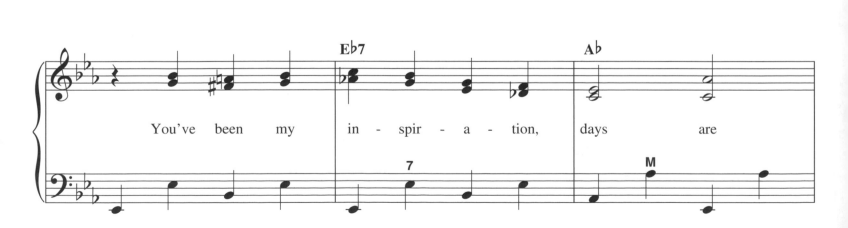

You've been my in - spir - a - tion, days are

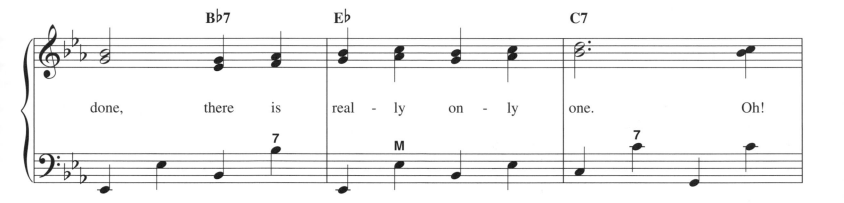

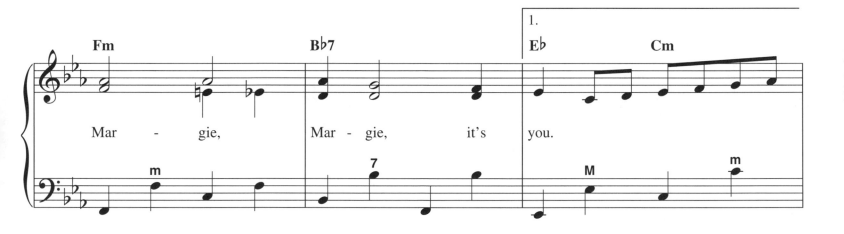

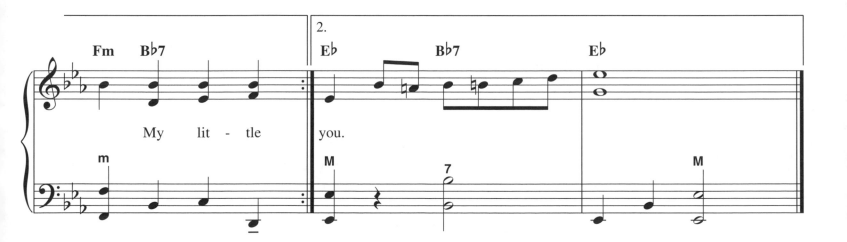

# I'M FOREVER BLOWING BUBBLES

Words and Music by JEAN KENBROVIN
and JOHN WILLIAM KELLETTE

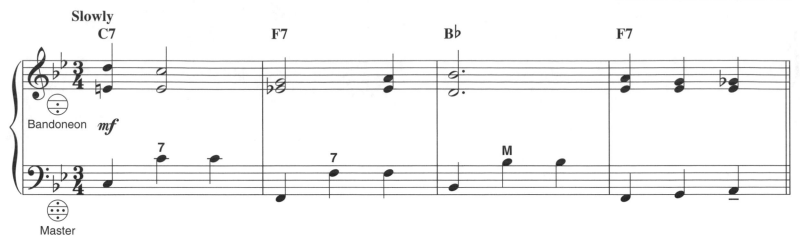

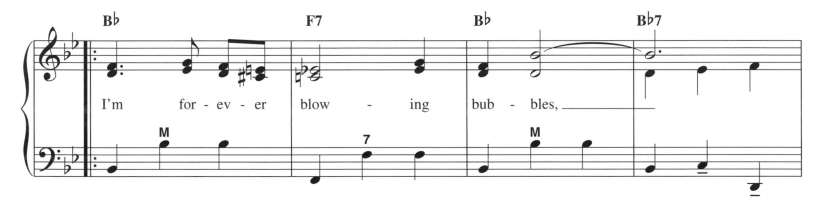

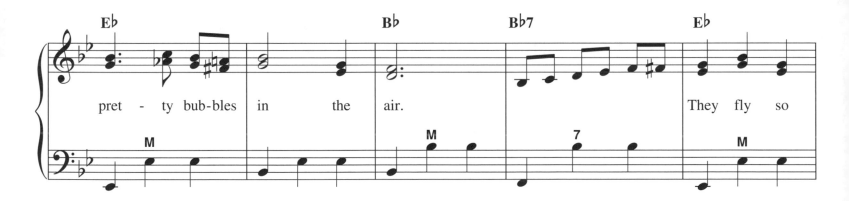

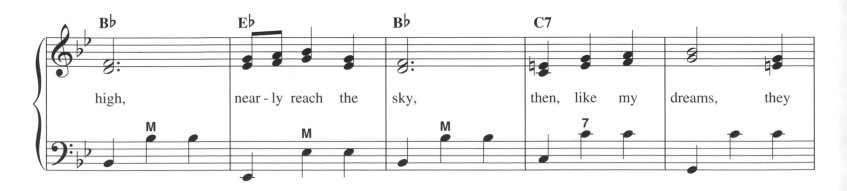

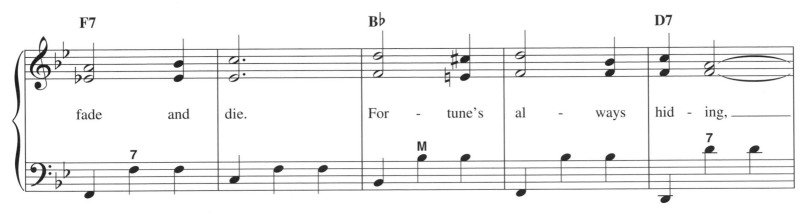

fade and die. For - tune's al - ways hid - ing, _____

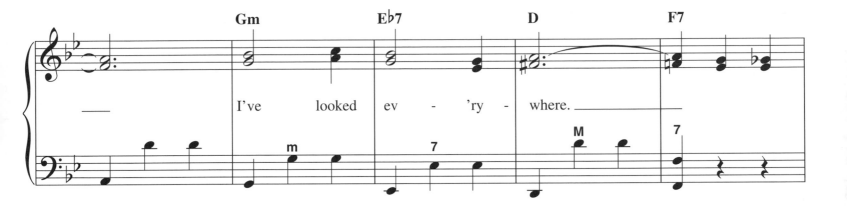

_____ I've looked ev - 'ry - where. _____

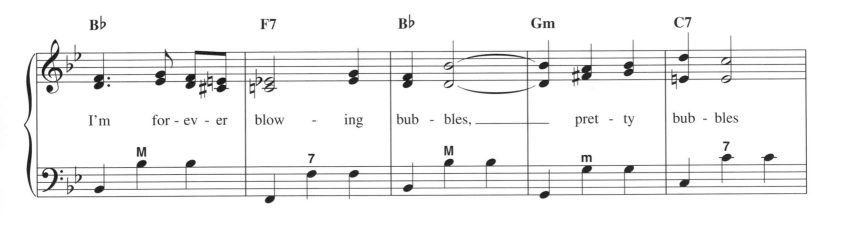

I'm for - ev - er blow - ing bub - bles, _____ pret - ty bub - bles

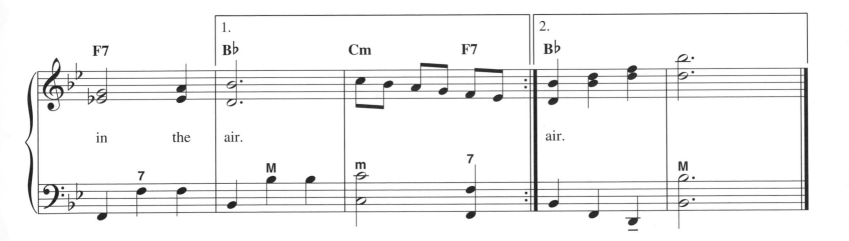

in the air.    air.

# I'VE BEEN WORKING ON THE RAILROAD

American Folksong

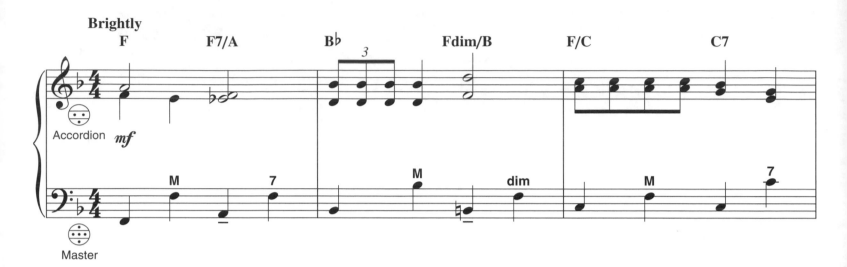

I've been work-ing on the rail - road,

all the live - long day. I've been work-ing on the

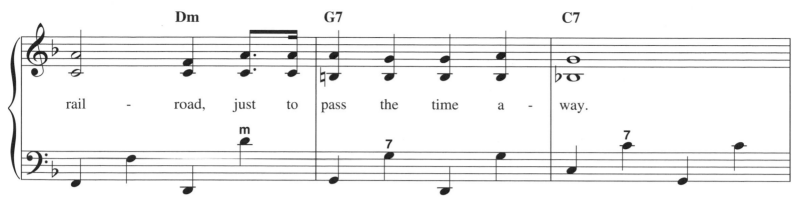

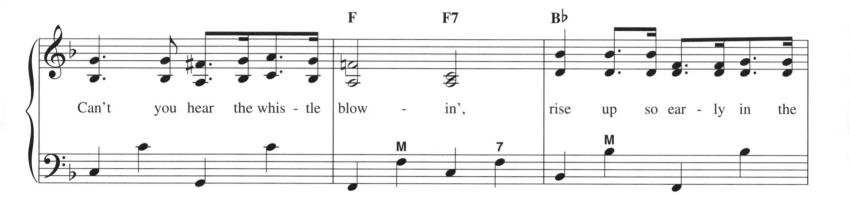

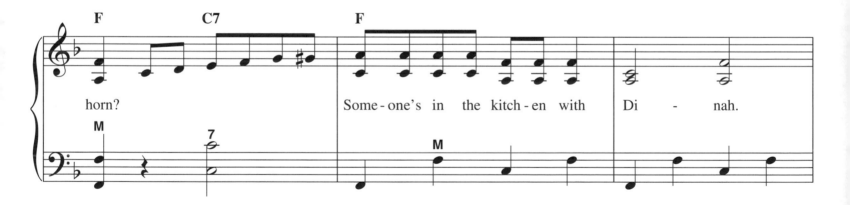

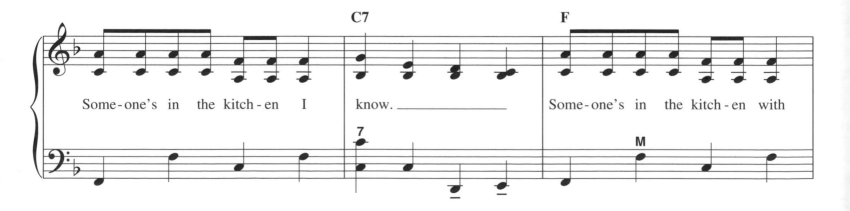

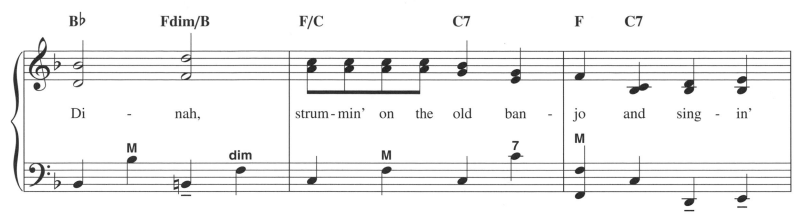

Di - nah, strum-min' on the old ban - jo and sing-in'

"Fee, fi, fid-dle-ee-i - o, fee, fi - fid-dle-ee-i -

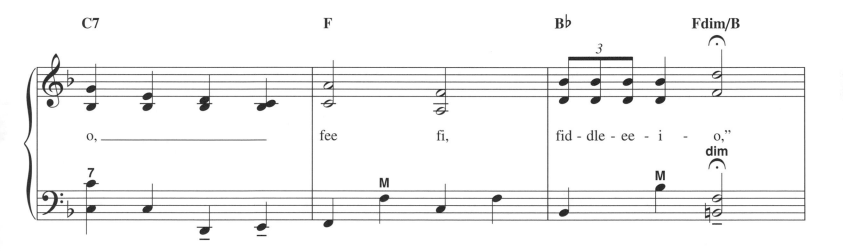

o, _____ fee fi, fid-dle-ee-i - o,"

strum-min' on the old ban - jo. jo.

# IN THE GOOD OLD SUMMERTIME

from IN THE GOOD OLD SUMMERTIME

Words by REN SHIELDS
Music by GEORGE EVANS

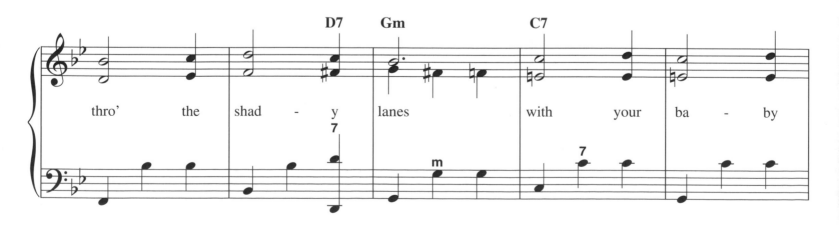

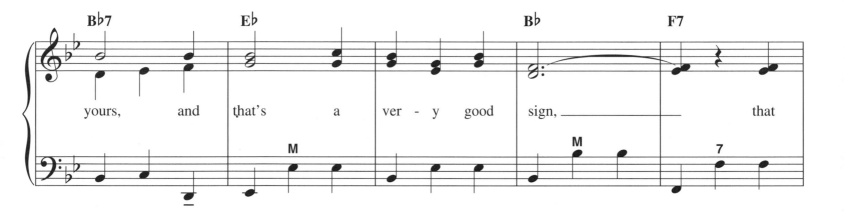

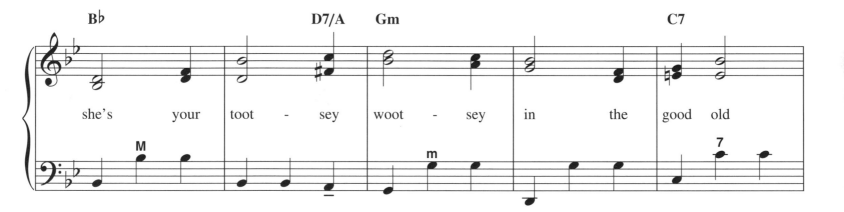

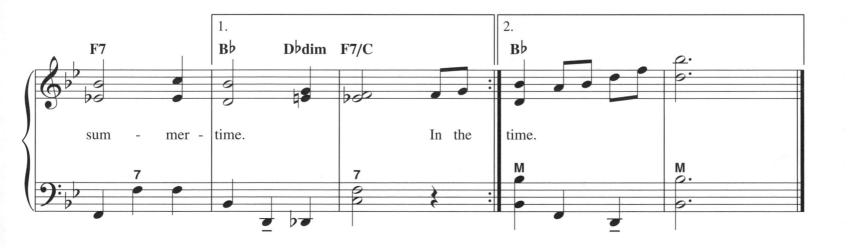

# LET ME CALL YOU SWEETHEART

Words by BETH SLATER WHITSON
Music by LEO FRIEDMAN

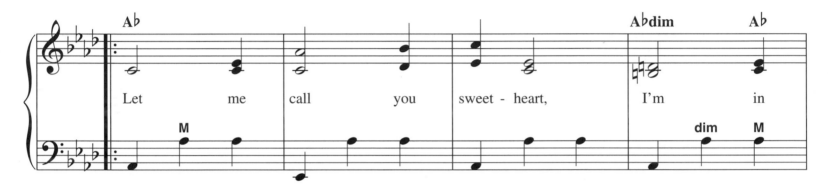

too. _____ Keep the love - light glow - ing

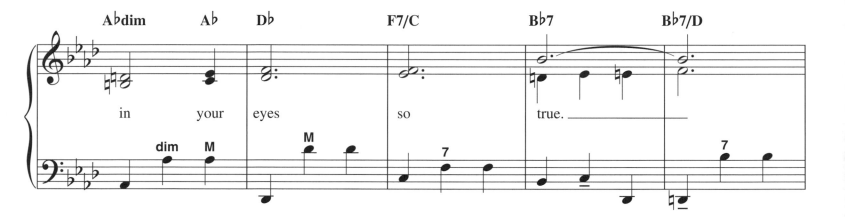

in your eyes so true. \_\_\_\_\_

Let me call you sweet - heart, I'm in love

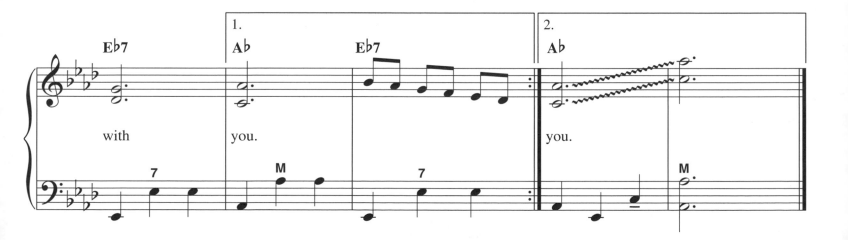

with you. you.

# MOONLIGHT BAY

Words by EDWARD MADDEN
Music by PERCY WENRICH

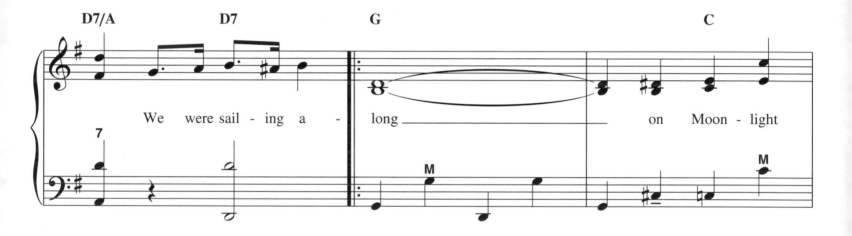

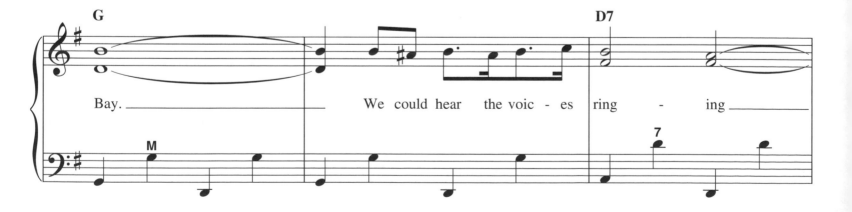

they seemed to say: "You have sto - len my

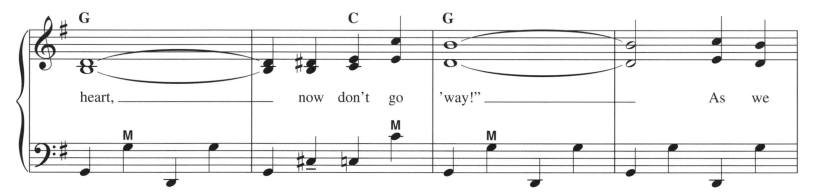

heart, _____ now don't go 'way!" _____ As we

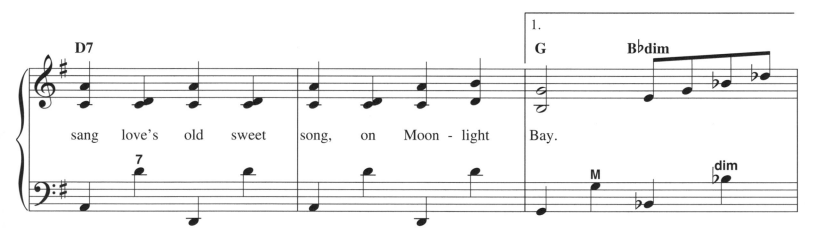

sang love's old sweet song, on Moon - light Bay.

1.

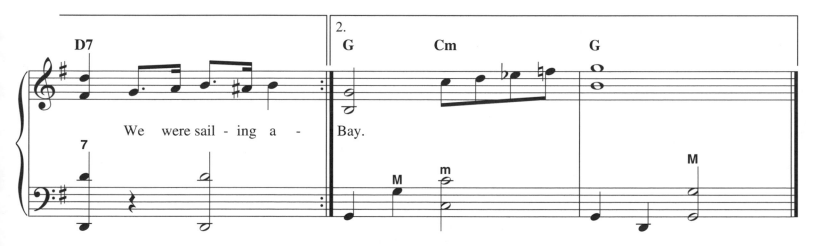

We were sail - ing a - Bay.

2.

# MY WILD IRISH ROSE

Words and Music by
CHAUNCEY OLCOTT

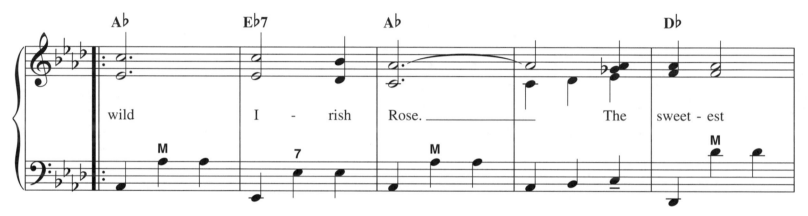

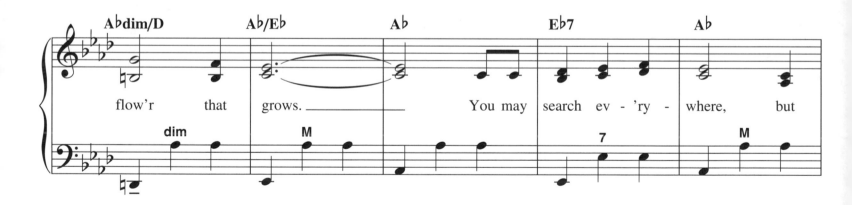

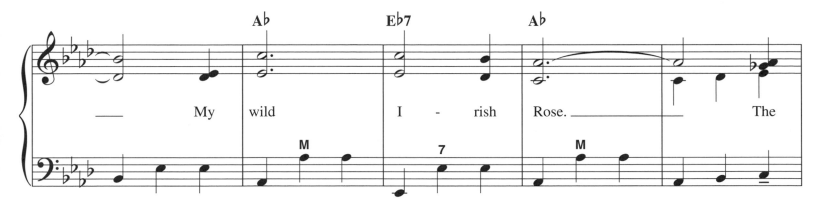

My wild I - rish Rose. ____ The

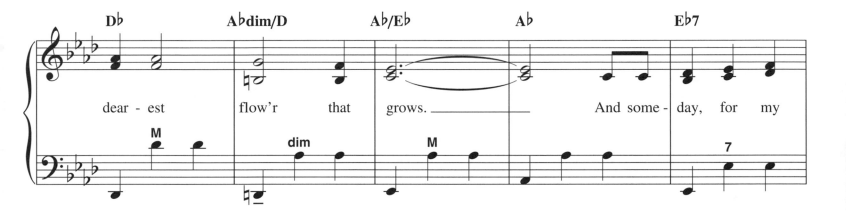

dear - est flow'r that grows. ____ And some - day, for my

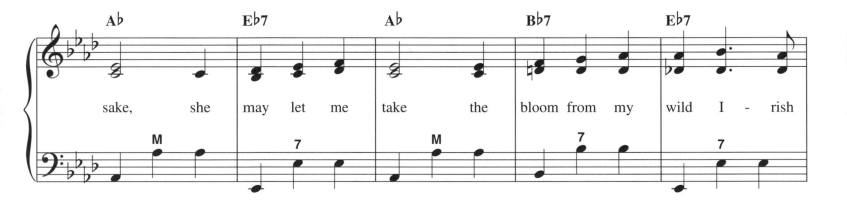

sake, she may let me take the bloom from my wild I - rish

1. Rose.

2. Rose.

# OH! SUSANNA

Words and Music by
STEPHEN C. FOSTER

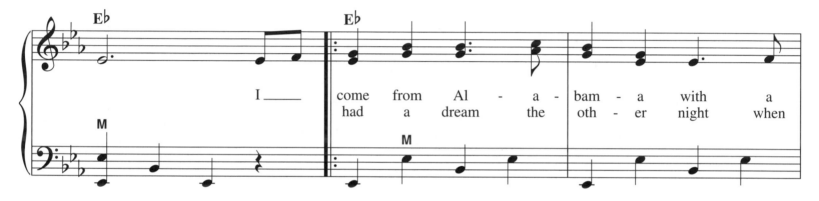

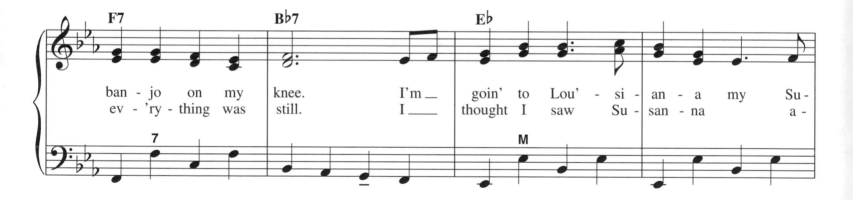

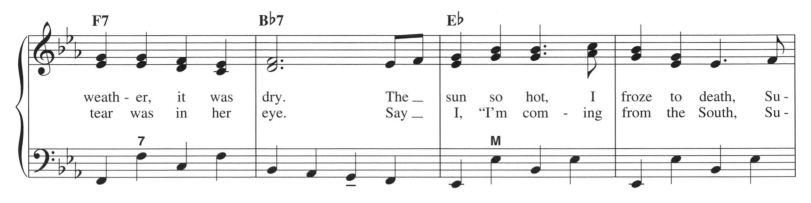

weath - er, it was dry. The __ sun so hot, I froze to death, Su -
tear was in her eye. Say __ I, "I'm com - ing from the South, Su -

san - na, don't you cry. }
san - na, don't you cry." }  Oh, Su - san - na, oh,

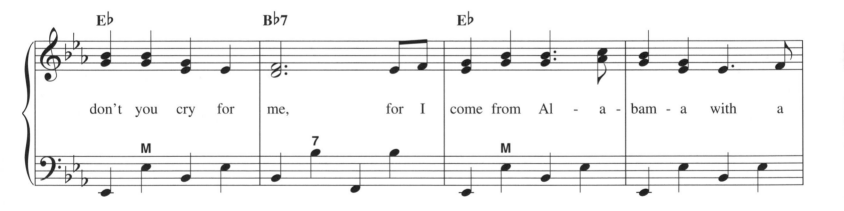

don't you cry for me, for I come from Al - a - bam - a with a

ban - jo on my knee. I _____ knee.

# ON TOP OF OLD SMOKY

Kentucky Mountain Folksong

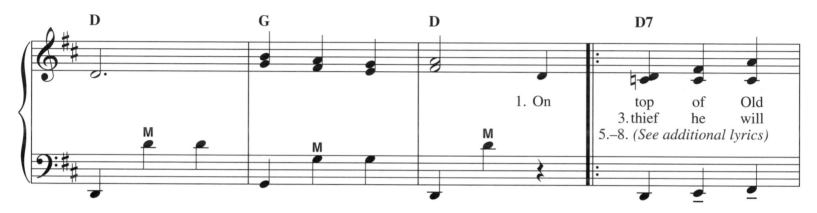

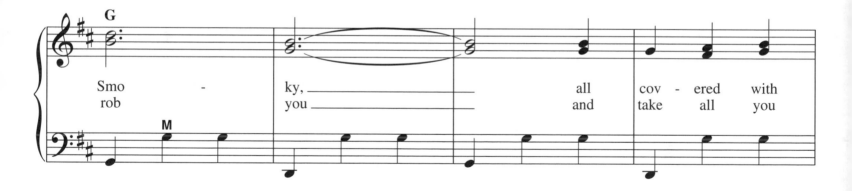

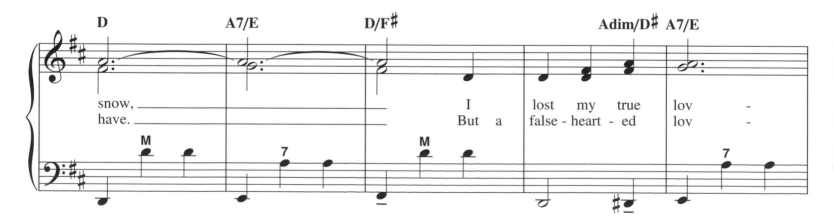

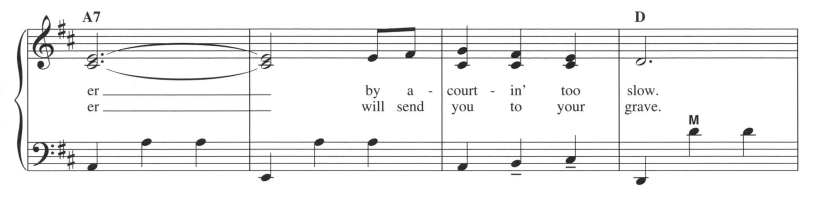

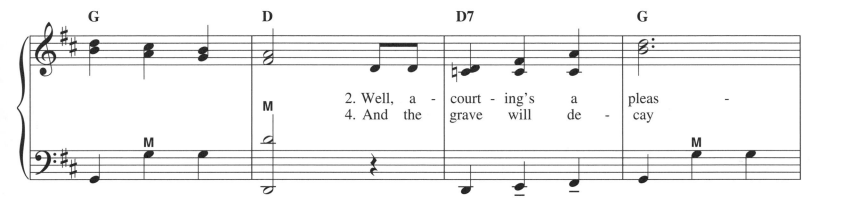

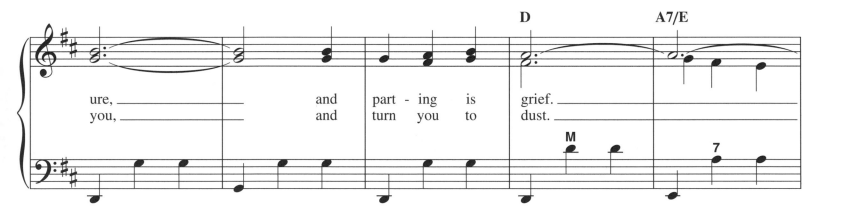

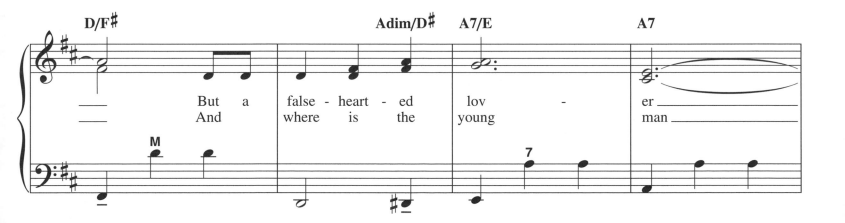

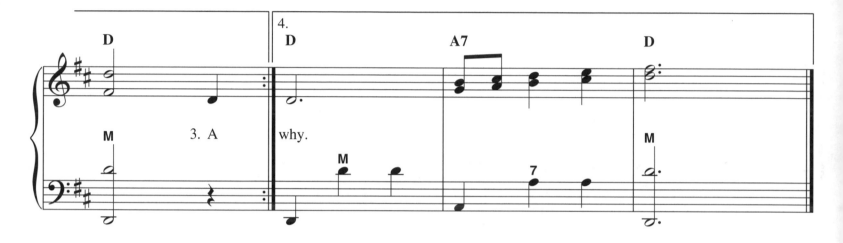

*Additional Lyrics*

5. They'll hug you and kiss you
   And tell you more lies
   Than the cross-ties on the railroad,
   Or the stars in the skies.

6. They'll tell you they love you,
   Just to give your heart ease.
   But the minute your back's turned,
   They'll court whom they please.

7. So come all you young maidens
   And listen to me.
   Never place your affection
   On a green willow tree.

8. For the leaves they will wither
   And the roots they will die,
   And your true love will leave you,
   And you'll never know why.

# PUT YOUR ARMS AROUND ME, HONEY

Words by JUNIE McCREE
Music by ALBERT VON TILZER

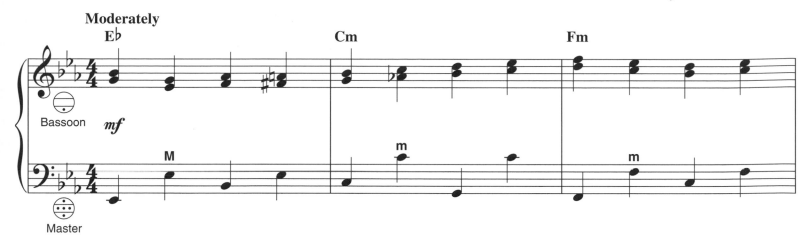

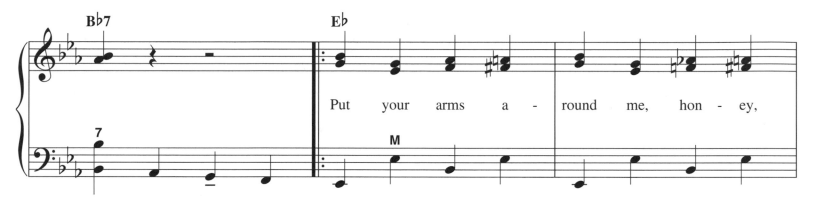

Put your arms a - round me, hon - ey,

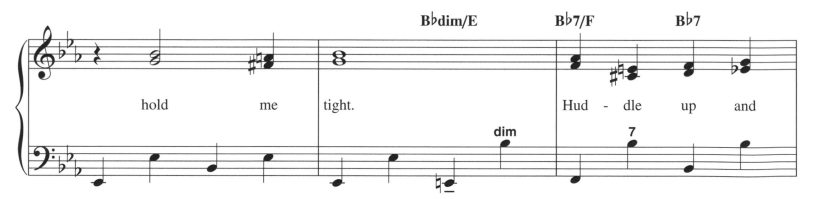

hold me tight. Hud - dle up and

cud - dle up with all your might.

Oh!      Oh!      Won't you roll those eyes,

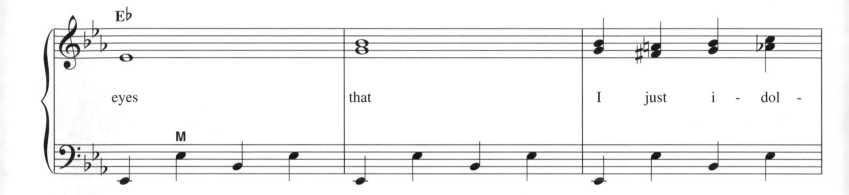

Eb

eyes      that      I   just   i   -   dol   -

M

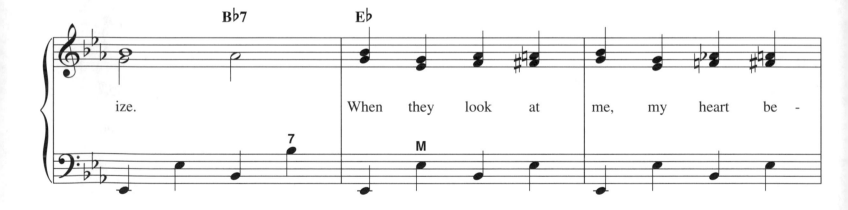

Bb7      Eb

ize.      When they look at   me,   my   heart   be   -

7      M

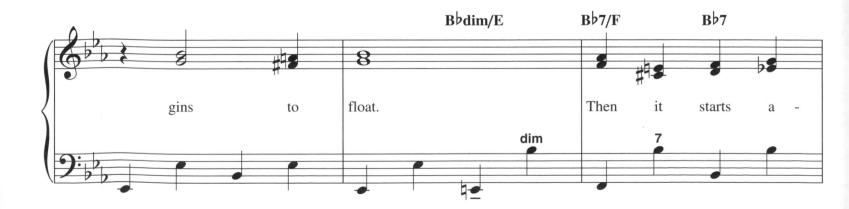

Bbdim/E      Bb7/F      Bb7

gins    to    float.      Then   it   starts   a   -

dim      7

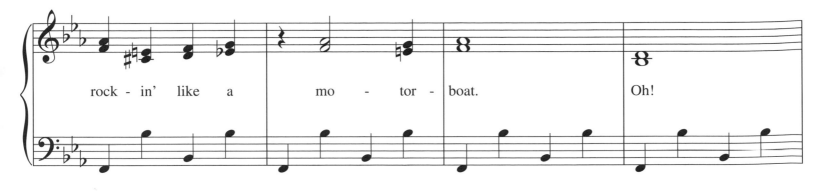

rock - in' like a mo - tor - boat. Oh!

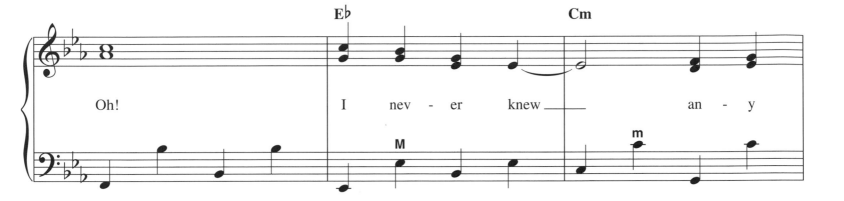

Oh! I nev - er knew an - y

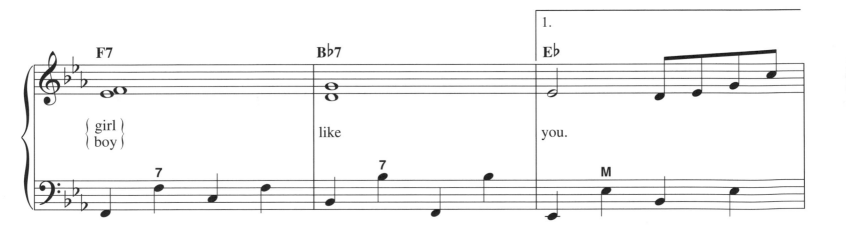

{ girl / boy } like you.

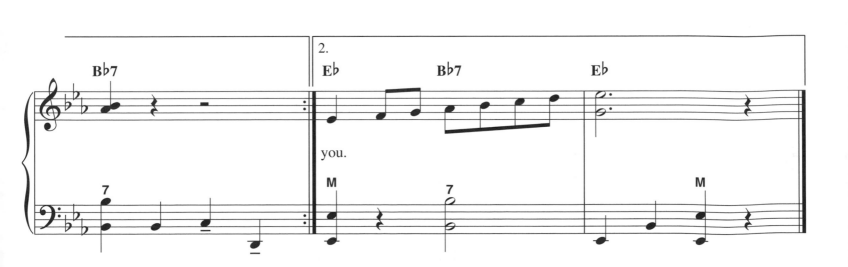

you.

# THE RED RIVER VALLEY

Traditional American Cowboy Song

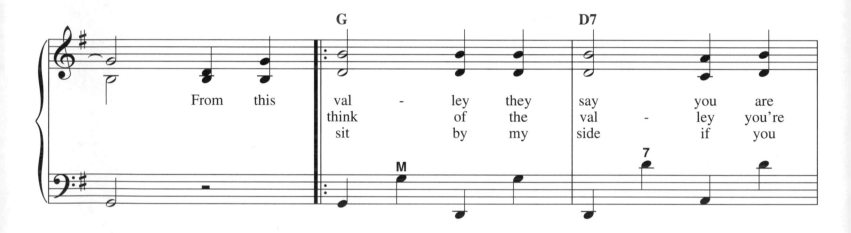

From this val - ley they say you are
think of the val - ley you're
sit by my side if you

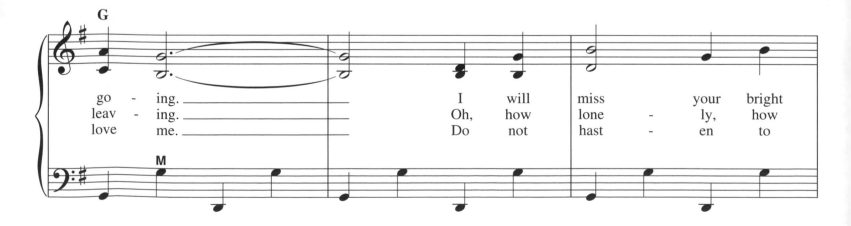

go - ing. _____ I will miss your bright
leav - ing. _____ Oh, how lone - ly, how
love me. _____ Do not hast - en to

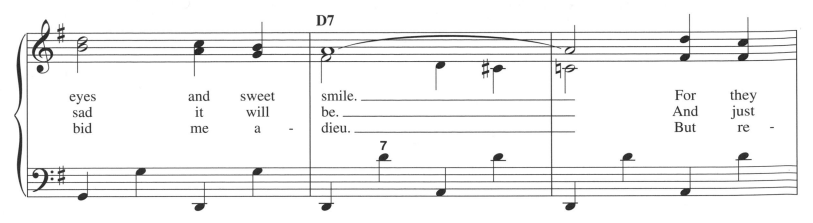
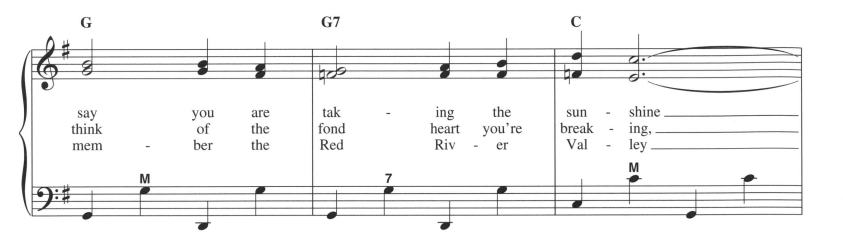
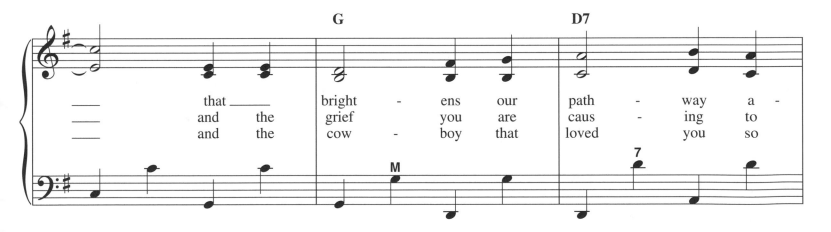

# SHE'LL BE COMIN' 'ROUND THE MOUNTAIN

Traditional

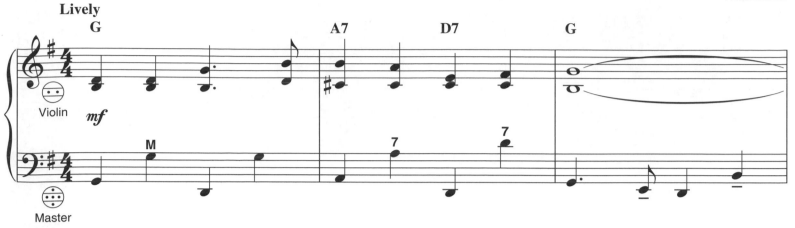

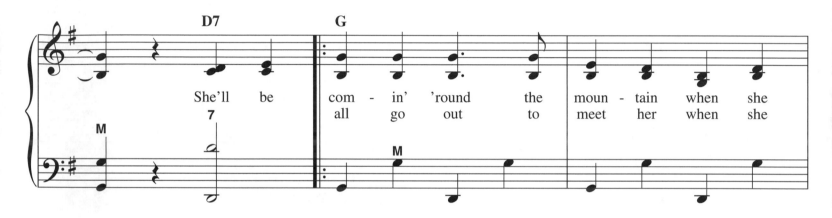

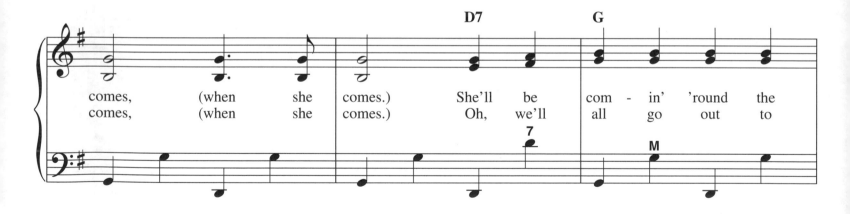

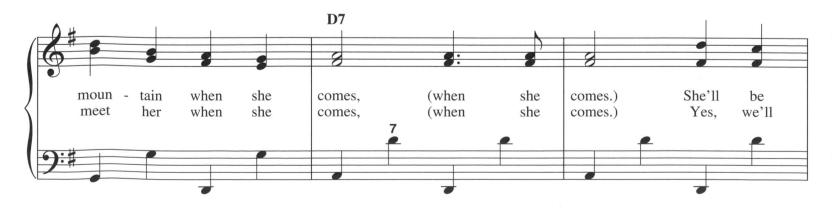

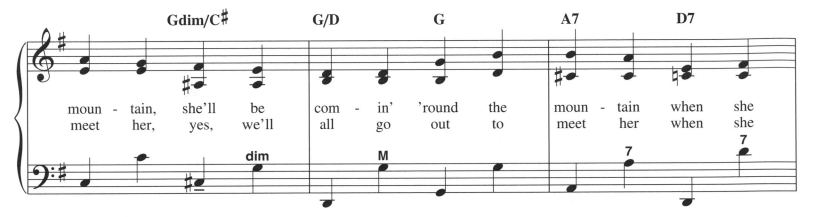

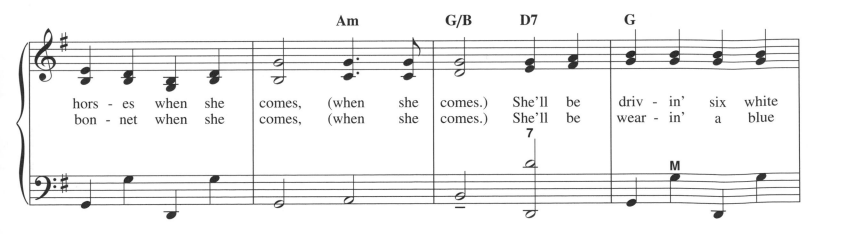

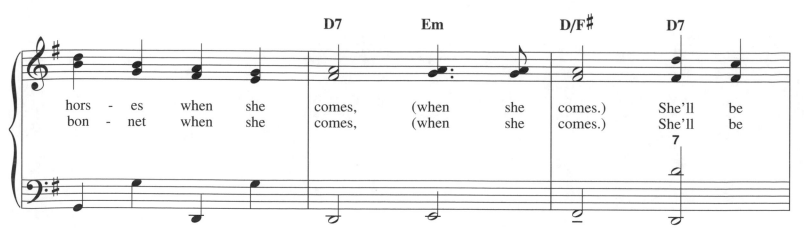

**D7**  **Em**  **D/F#**  **D7**

hors - es when she comes, (when she comes.) She'll be
bon - net when she comes, (when she comes.) She'll be

**G**  **G7**  **C**

driv - in' six white hors - es, she'll be driv - in' six white
wear - in' a blue bon - net, she'll be wear - in' a blue

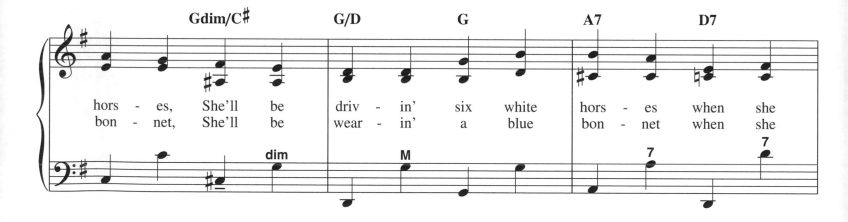

**Gdim/C#**  **G/D**  **G**  **A7**  **D7**

hors - es, She'll be driv - in' six white hors - es when she
bon - net, She'll be wear - in' a white bon - net when she

1.
**G**  **Ddim/G#**  **D7/A**  **D7**

2.
**G**

comes.                    Oh, we'll      comes.

# TAKE ME OUT TO THE BALL GAME

Words by JACK NORWORTH
Music by ALBERT VON TILZER

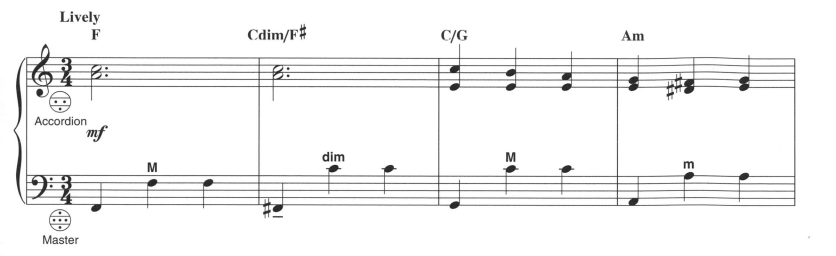

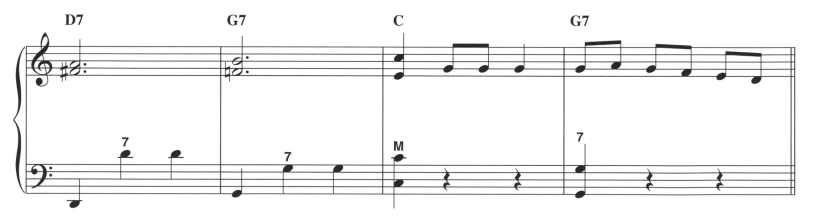

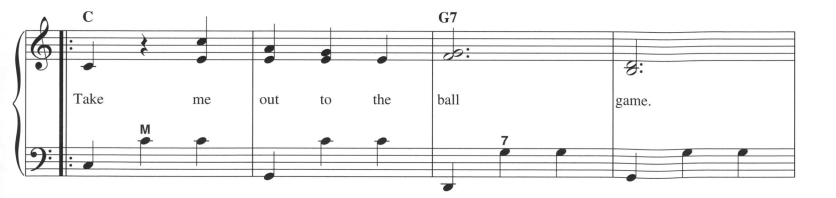

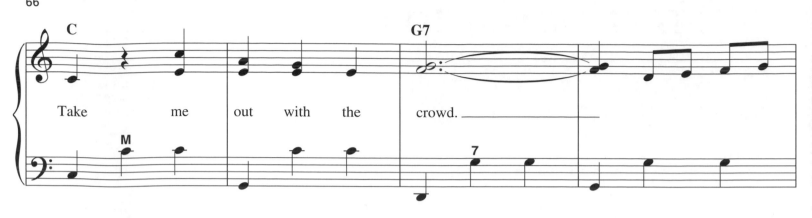

Take me out with the crowd.

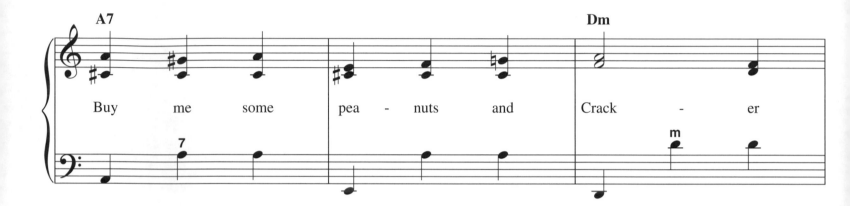

Buy me some pea - nuts and Crack - er

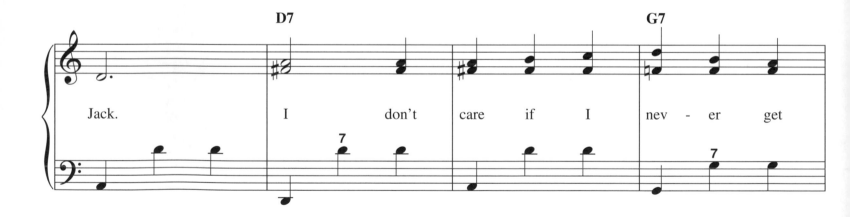

Jack. I don't care if I nev - er get

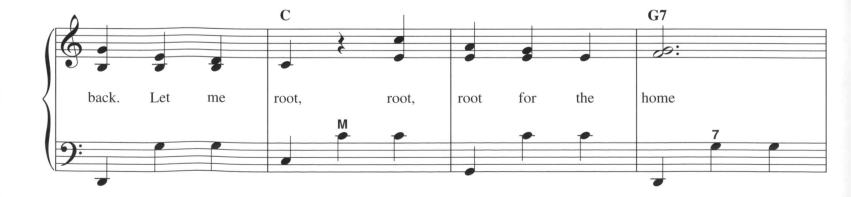

back. Let me root, root, root for the home

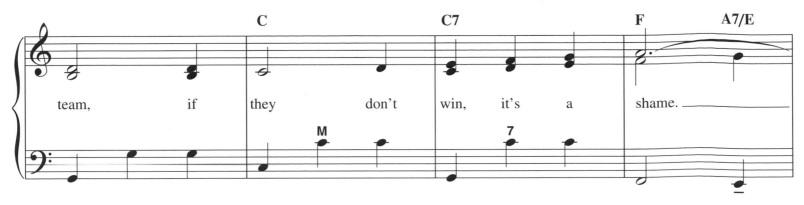

team, if they don't win, it's a shame. _____

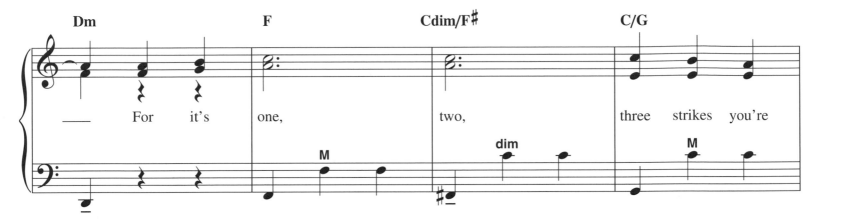

_____ For it's one, two, three strikes you're

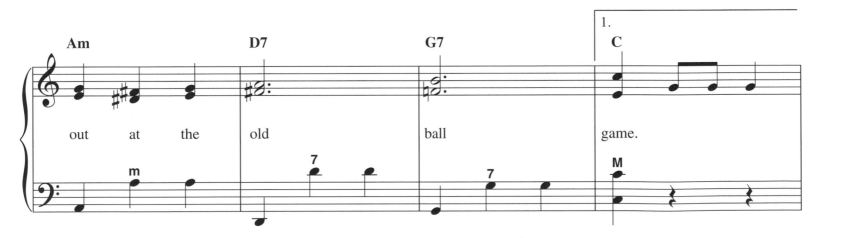

out at the old ball game.

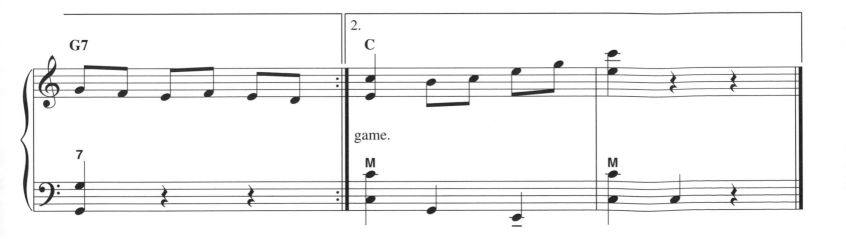

game.

# SHINE ON, HARVEST MOON

Words by JACK NORWORTH
Music by NORA BAYES
and JACK NORWORTH

Oh, shine on, shine on, har-vest moon _____ up in the

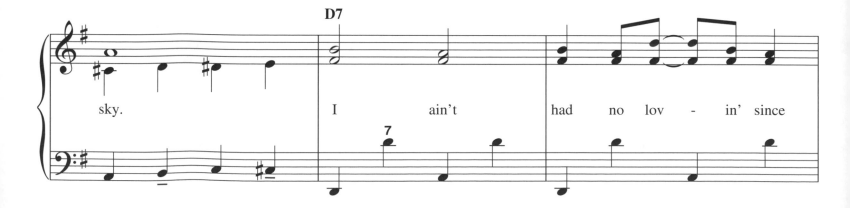

sky. I ain't had no lov - in' since

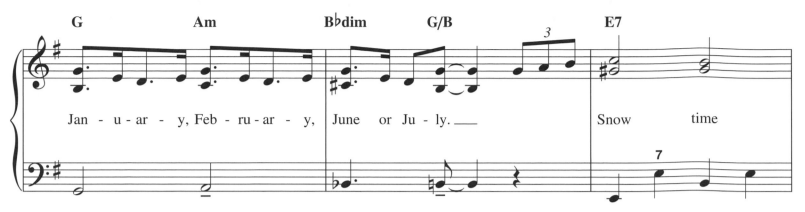

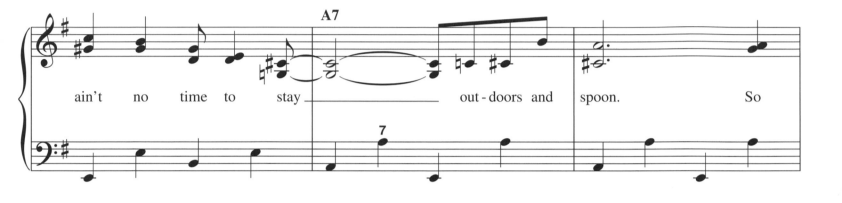

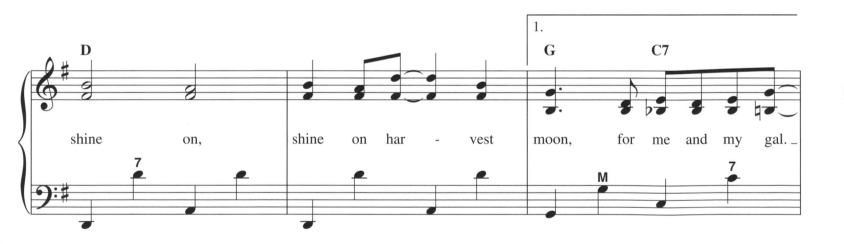

# WHEN THE SAINTS GO MARCHING IN

Traditional

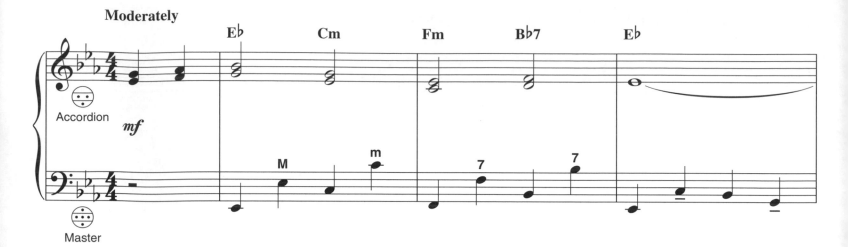

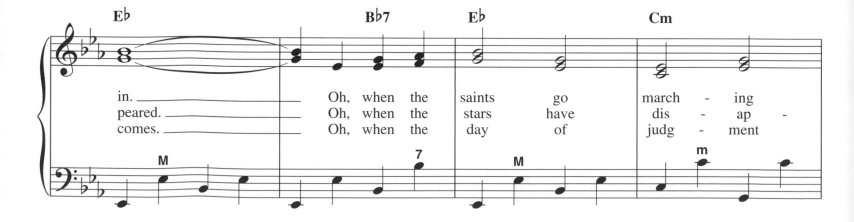

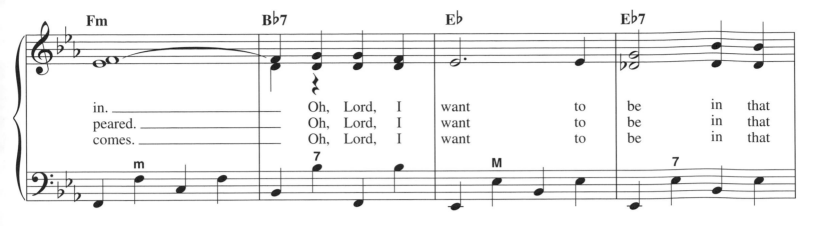

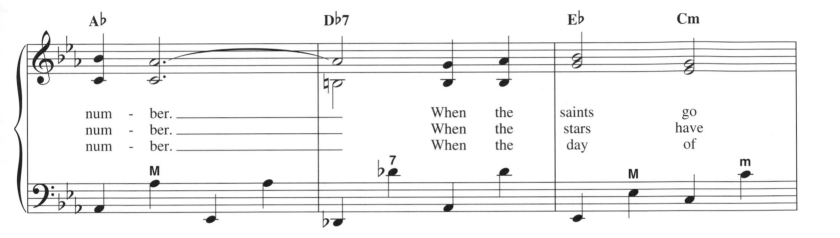

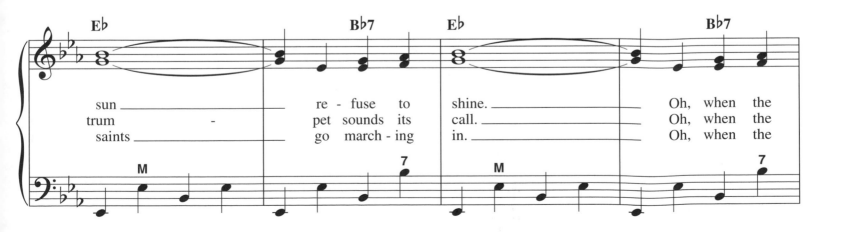

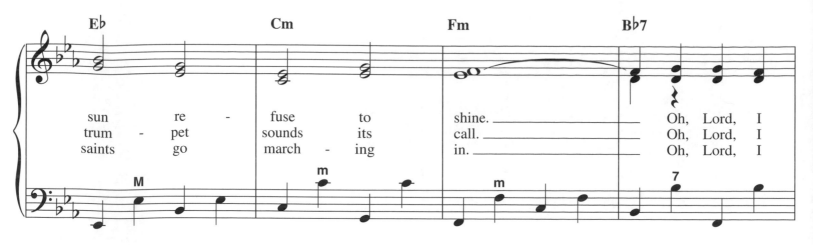

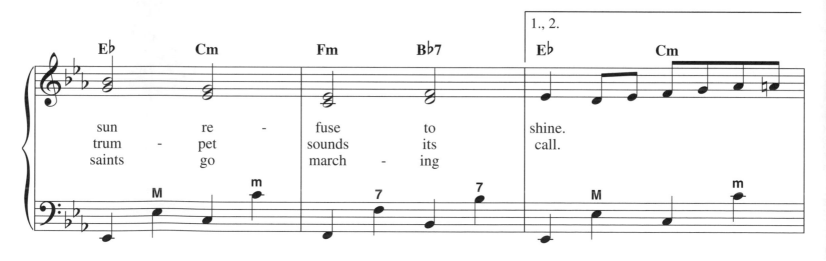

# WHEN YOU WORE A TULIP
## (And I Wore a Big Red Rose)

Words by JACK MAHONEY
Music by PERCY WENRICH

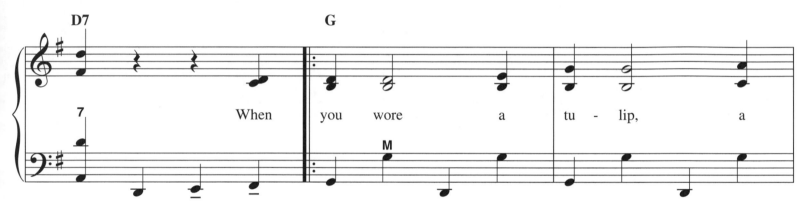

When you wore a tu - lip, a

sweet yel - low tu - lip, and I wore a

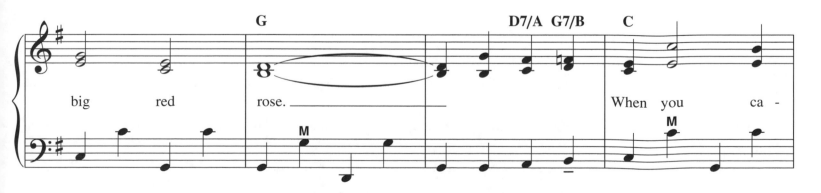

big red rose. _____ When you ca -

ressed me,    'twas    then    heav  -  en    blessed me,    what    a

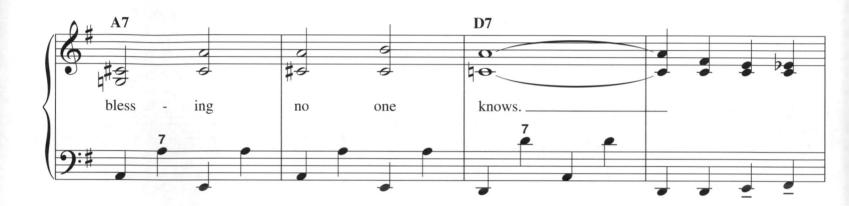

bless  -  ing    no    one    knows.

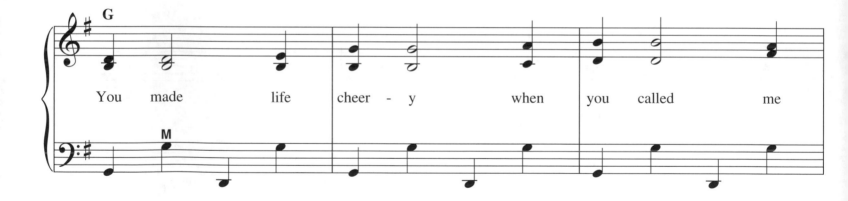

You    made    life    cheer  -  y    when    you    called    me

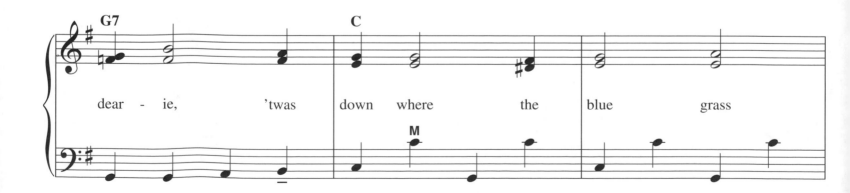

dear  -  ie,    'twas    down    where    the    blue    grass

grows. _____ Your lips were sweet - er than

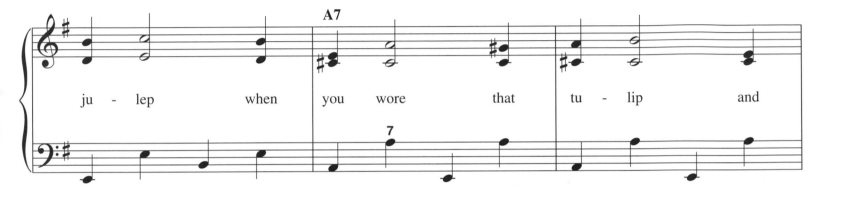

ju – lep when you wore that tu – lip and

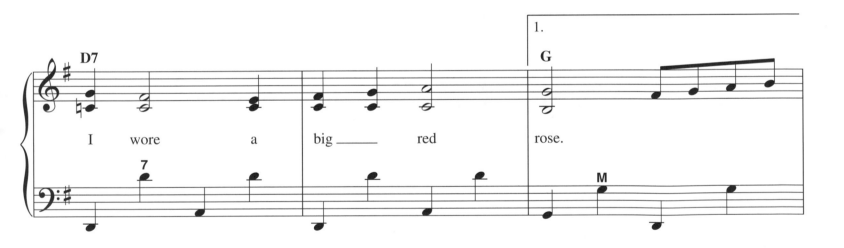

I wore a big ___ red rose.

When rose.

# YANKEE DOODLE

Traditional

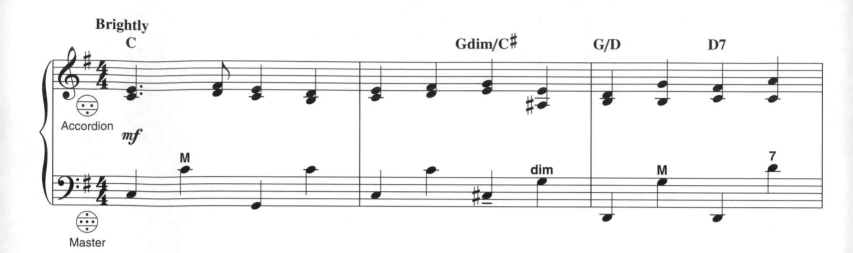

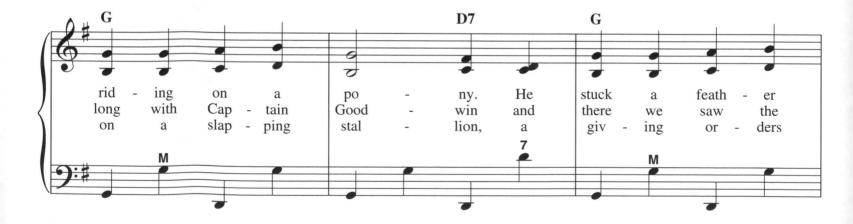

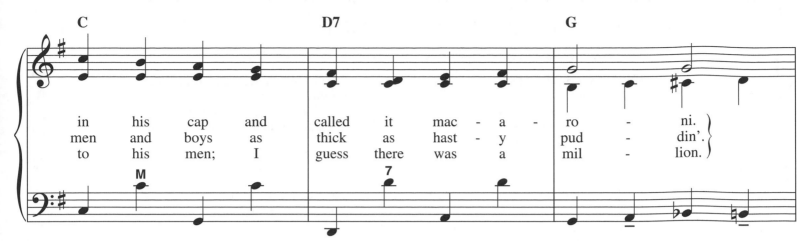

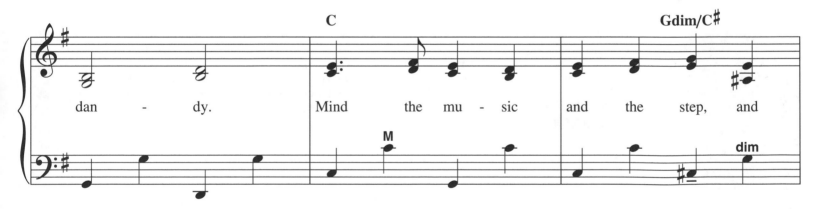

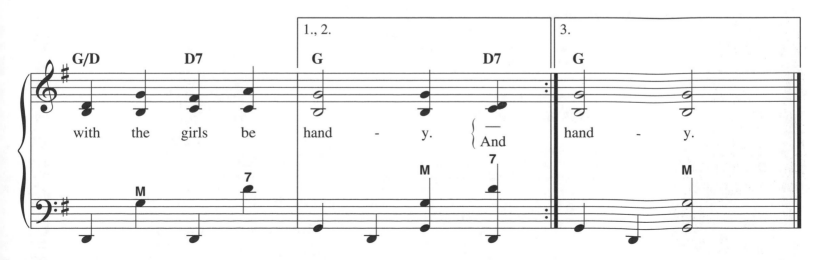

# A COLLECTION OF ALL-TIME FAVORITES FOR ACCORDION

## ACCORDION FAVORITES
*arr. Gary Meisner*

16 all-time favorites, arranged for accordion, including: Can't Smile Without You • Could I Have This Dance • Endless Love • Memory • Sunrise, Sunset • I.O.U. • and more.
00359012 ................................................................$10.95

## ALL-TIME FAVORITES FOR ACCORDION
*arr. Gary Meisner*

20 must-know standards arranged for accordions. Includes: Ain't Misbehavin' • Autumn Leaves • Crazy • Hello, Dolly! • Hey, Good Lookin' • Moon River • Speak Softly, Love • Unchained Melody • The Way We Were • Zip-A-Dee-Doo-Dah • and more.
00311088 ................................................................$10.95

## THE BEATLES GREATEST HITS FOR ACCORDION

15 of the Beatles greatest hits arranged for accordion. Includes: Lucy in the Sky with Diamonds • A Hard Day's Night • Yellow Submarine • All My Loving • Yesterday • Michelle • Hey Jude • more.
00359121 ................................................................$12.99

## BROADWAY FAVORITES
*arr. Ken Kotwitz*

A collection of 17 wonderful show songs, including: Don't Cry for Me Argentina • Getting to Know You • If I Were a Rich Man • Oklahoma • People Will Say We're in Love • We Kiss in a Shadow.
00490157 ................................................................$9.95

## CHRISTMAS SONGS FOR ACCORDION

17 holiday hits, including: The Chipmunk Song • Frosty the Snow Man • A Holly Jolly Christmas • Jingle-Bell Rock • Pretty Paper • Rudolph the Red-Nosed Reindeer.
00359477 ................................................................$8.99

## CONTEMPORARY HITS FOR ACCORDION
*arr. Gary Meisner*

15 songs, including: I Left My Heart in San Francisco • Just the Way You Are • Longer • September Morn • Somewhere Out There • Through the Years • and more.
00359491 ................................................................$9.95

## DISNEY MOVIE FAVORITES

Students will love playing these 12 songs from the Disney favorites *Aladdin, Beauty and the Beast*, and *The Little Mermaid*. Songs include: Under the Sea • Be Our Guest • A Whole New World • and more!
00311632 ................................................................$9.95

## ITALIAN SONGS FOR ACCORDION
*arr. Gary Meisner*

17 favorite Italian standards arranged for accordion, including: Carnival of Venice • Ciribiribin • Come Back to Sorrento • Funiculi, Funicula • La donna è mobile • La Spagnola • 'O Sole Mio • Santa Lucia • Tarantella • and more.
00311089 ................................................................$9.95

## LATIN FAVORITES FOR ACCORDION
*arr. Gary Meisner*

20 Latin favorites, including: Bésame Mucho (Kiss Me Much) • The Girl from Ipanema • How Insensitive (Insensatez) • Perfidia • Spanish Eyes • So Nice (Summer Samba) • and more.
00310932 ................................................................$10.99

## THE SONGS OF ANDREW LLOYD WEBBER FOR ACCORDION

10 of his best, including: All I Ask of You • Any Dream Will Do • As If We Never Said Goodbye • I Don't Know How to Love Him • Love Changes Everything • The Music of the Night • Old Deuteronomy • Think of Me • Unexpected Song • With One Look.
00310152 ................................................................$10.95

## POLKA FAVORITES
*arr. Kenny Kotwitz*

An exciting new collection of 16 songs, including: Beer Barrel Polka • Liechtensteiner Polka • My Melody of Love • Paloma Blanca • Pennsylvania Polka • Too Fat Polka • and more.
00311573 ................................................................$10.95

## WALTZ FAVORITES
*arr. Kenny Kotwitz*

Accordion arrangements of 17 classic waltzes, including: Alice Blue Gown • I Love You Truly • I Wonder Who's Kissing Her Now • I'll Be with You in Apple Blossom Time • Let Me Call You Sweetheart • Let the Rest of the World Go By • My Buddy • and more.
00310576 ................................................................$9.95

## LAWRENCE WELK'S POLKA FOLIO

More than 50 famous polkas, schottisches and waltzes arranged for piano and accordion, including: Blue Eyes • Budweiser Polka • Clarinet Polka • Cuckoo Polka • The Dove Polka • Draw One Polka • Gypsy Polka • Helena Polka • International Waltzes • Let's Have Another One • Schnitzelbank • Shuffle Schottische • Squeeze Box Polka • Waldteufel Waltzes • and more.
00123218 ................................................................$10.95

Prices, contents & availability
subject to change without notice.

Disney artwork & characters © Disney Enterprises, Inc.

FOR MORE INFORMATION,
SEE YOUR LOCAL MUSIC DEALER,
OR WRITE TO:

## HAL•LEONARD®
CORPORATION
7777 W. BLUEMOUND RD. P.O. BOX 13819
MILWAUKEE, WISCONSIN 53213

Visit Hal Leonard Online at **www.halleonard.com**

1110

# HAL•LEONARD ACCORDION PLAY•ALONG

The Accordion Play-Along series features custom accordion arrangements with CD tracks recorded by a live band (accordion, bass and drums). There are two audio tracks for each song – a full performance for listening, plus a separate backing track which lets you be the soloist! The CD is playable on any CD player, and is also enhanced so Mac and PC users can adjust the recording to any tempo without changing the pitch!

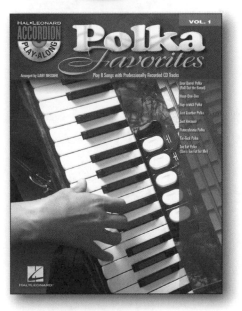

## 1. POLKA FAVORITES

*arr. Gary Meisner*

Beer Barrel Polka (Roll Out the Barrel) • Hoop-Dee-Doo • Hop-scotch Polka • Just Another Polka • Just Because • Pennsylvania Polka • Tic-Tock Polka • Too Fat Polka (She's Too Fat for Me).
00701705 Book/CD Pack........................................................................$14.99

## 2. ALL-TIME HITS

*arr. Gary Meisner*

Edelweiss • Fly Me to the Moon (In Other Words) • I Left My Heart in San Francisco • It's a Small World • Moon River • More (Ti Guarderò Nel Cuore) • Poinciana (Song of the Tree) • When I'm Sixty-Four.
00701706 Book/CD Pack........................................................................$14.99

## 3. CLASSIC SONGS

*arr. Gary Meisner*

Carnival of Venice • Ciribiribin • Come Back to Sorrento • Fascination (Valse Tzigane) • Funiculi, Funicula • I Love You Truly • In the Good Old Summertime • Melody of Love • Peg O' My Heart • When Irish Eyes Are Smiling.
00701707 Book/CD Pack........................................................................$14.99

## 4. CHRISTMAS SONGS

*arr. Gary Meisner*

Frosty the Snow Man • Have Yourself a Merry Little Christmas • Here Comes Santa Claus (Right down Santa Claus Lane) • The Most Wonderful Time of the Year • Rudolph the Red-Nosed Reindeer • Santa Claus Is Comin' to Town • Silver Bells • Winter Wonderland.
00101770 Book/CD Pack........................................................................$14.99

# HAL•LEONARD® CORPORATION

7777 W. Bluemound Rd. P.O. Box 13819 Milwaukee, WI 53213